Mama Hawa

THE STORY OF PARAMOUNT CHIEF OF IMPERRI CHIEFDOM, SIERRA LEONE

Sylvanus Kpanabom

To Chief Beah Hiteh and Chief Baun.
To my daughter, Ndaneh Frimpong.

Acknowledgments

I would like to thank President Julius Maada Bio of Sierra Leone.

My gratitude I would like to extend to Chief Beah Hiteh from Imperri Chiefdom and Daniel Wilberforce Flickenger, who was an American missionary.

I would like to thank Darlene Oakley who has edited and looked after this story about my sister.

Thank you to those who provided photos. Not all were able to be included in this book, but I am grateful for your support.

And last, but certainly not least, thank you to Doug and Nancy Court and their family.

Pictures from top left to bottom: Mama Hawa; Mama Hawa & young man; and current president of Sierra Leone: Julius Maada Bio.

Pictures from top left to bottom: Mama Hawa; Queen Elizabeth II dancing with Sir Martin Margai; and Mama Hawa

Preface

The events that shaped the life of Mama Hawa, Paramount Chief, Hawa Kpanabom, originated from her father who arranged for his daughter to be brought up by relatives in Bo Town. She returned home to Kpangbama as a young woman and got married to Dr. Milton Margai.

Dr. Margai, a medical doctor, was a political party organiser. He became a party leader of Sierra Leone's People's Party (S.L.P.P.), Prime Minister, Head of State when Sierra Leone became an independent state and, eventually a knight in the British Commonwealth of Nations. He was knighted by Queen Elizabeth II.

Mama Hawa was not a mere housewife. She participated in national and local politics by campaigning with her husband, attending meetings, and entertaining politicians. She got elected Paramount Chief of the Imperri Chiefdom in the early eighties.

Chapter 1: Paramount Chief

The Election

A crowd of thousands had gathered in the court to await the 1985 Sierra Leone election results. The Provincial Secretary walked out of the Courtroom with the results.

He greeted the crowd then proceeded with the announcement of the election results: "In the Southern Province of Sierra Leone, Bonthe District, Imperri Chiefdom, the Paramount Chief elect is Madam Hawa Kpanabom."

There was a clash of reactions from the crowd. There was swearing and insulting of the chiefdom people on one side and on another wailing and despair, while on still another the victors were jubilant, the winners sang victory songs as they danced around the town. The Regent Chief lost no time in deploying more security personnel to protect the Chief elect and the Government Officials that had conducted the election as they hurried to leave.

Still, joy, happiness, singing and dancing of the Chief elect did spread to every corner of the town.

Security personnel cautiously guided Madam Kpanabom to her residence. She quickly discarded her ornamental robe, gold bangle, and gold necklaces. She invited the Regent Chief inside. "You are still the chief in this town. Please help me feed this crowd that have been around here for over a week. Take chickens, goats, sheep, cows and any food items in my compound suitable to feed this crowd. Let every household in Kpangbama have pots boiling to feed this crowd. I am going to the kitchen, myself, with my helpers."

In a short time, food was available for all that wanted to eat and take away. Madam Hawa made free food available in Kpangbama for a whole week for those who needed it.

Partners in Politics

The faction that was crying and lamenting when the election results were announced lost one of their members through a sudden heart attack. They were unable to save him.

Candidates and their supporters take the highest risks and spend a lot of money during Chiefdom elections. Some candidates will go to the extent of selling most of their family's valuables or assets—guns, machinery, plantations and land—in order to raise funds for election expenditure. If they are lucky to win and become Paramount Chief, which is a position for life, they will be able to generate more wealth during their lifetime. But, when they find themselves on the losing end, it becomes a problem for the entire family and their supporters. The candidate today and his adult children might not have the possibility of witnessing another Chiefdom Election. When a young Chief is elected, one would expect him or her to rule for probably the next thirty-five years.

There is one and only one position for a Paramount Chief in a Chiefdom. But there are other lucrative positions in every Chiefdom that are open for those interested in the chief business such as Village Head, Town Chief, Tribal Authority, Section Chief and his or her assistant. The positions of Chiefdom Speakers and Court Chairperson are elected positions. A good citizen, a land holder, particularly someone who had qualified to contest for Paramount Chieftaincy can get into any of these positions with relative ease.

The group that was swearing and insulting the Chiefdom people, referring to the Tribal Authorities of Imperri as primitive and fetishistic, and that would never leave their old way, following the announcement of the election results, was attacked by the security force and the Chiefdom People. Some arrests were made, and the rest quickly disappeared from town.

The group were supporters of a United States college professor, an education doctor, who genuinely qualified to contest the Chieftaincy in the Imperri Chiefdom. In the two hundred years prior, Christian and European traders had considerable influence on Chieftaincy along the Sherbro River, and in particular, in the Bonthe District. In some Chiefdoms, American missionaries had assisted their faithful members in becoming Chiefs in order to promote Christianity. On the other hand, successful European businessmen sought to dominate a suitable business domain through marriage. It is not unusual for a successful businessman or his son to get married to the daughter of a Chief.

Newcomers, Merchants, and Traders

In the eighteenth century, European traders and American missionaries were completely integrated into the Chieftaincy of Imperri. The Mission had a residence, hospital, church and school in Gbangbai. They educated the children of Chiefs, merchants and settlers who were British. During this time, they were expanding further into the Hinterland with the Church business. In order to provide protection, support, and create business opportunities for the new settlers along the Sherbro River, the Government in Freetown built a residence and police barracks in Kpangbama to locate the first Commissioner in the Hinterland. The resident Commissioner in the Hinterland and the American missionaries assisted the newcomers to settle further in the Hinterland and take advantage of the economic opportunities in the area. These new settlers did increase the food and commodity production that was in high demand for the export market.

The Resident Commissioner in the Hinterland and his large police force were not limited to only assisting newcomers, tradesmen, and merchants to settle, but they also assumed administrative duties and public works in economically viable areas where the newcomers settled. Although they employed the natives to do what they wanted done, they completely ignored the authority of the native Chiefs. Those policemen, in particular, who were foreigners, fully armed, did not have any regard for the Chiefs. They considered the Chiefs illiterate and fetishistic. However, they do help with the construction of roads and bridges that allowed for the safe passage of food and commodities. They also introduced the mail carrying system along the Sherbro River, and into the Hinterland as there, there were merchants, tradesmen, and missionaries.

Businesses did prosper along the Sherbro River. From there, the enterprising merchants and traders went as far into the Hinterland as they could to get commodities for the export market. While these people prospered and became wealthy, the natives and their Chiefs became poorer. The administrative system instituted by the Resident Commissioner made the Chiefs and their subjects powerless, while the newcomers took control in all the areas in which they were allowed to settle. The natives and their Chiefs became disgruntled.

The Sherbro-Mende people started to express their dissatisfaction openly to government officials and the new settlers by creating the Poro Society to prevent access to some productive areas. Some palm fruit and palm cannel collecting areas became strictly reserved to Chiefs and natives that were Poro Society members. The resident Commissioner resisted this approach of the Chiefs; alternatively, he gave the command that Poro Society restrictions be removed from all productive areas. Where these restrictions of the Poro Society were not removed, he permitted the businessmen to go anywhere they wanted to operate as long as they were protected by the police.

The conflict between the settlers and the natives along the Sherbro River, and even much further into the Hinterland, persisted. Neither the Resident Commissioner nor the Government in Freetown showed willingness to solve this problem. They thought the problem would go away if businesses continued to prosper. Unfortunately, the situation continued to deteriorate, particularly in the Hinterland, where Poro Society attacks became more frequent, and some businessmen started to pull out, and go back to Freetown.

The aggression of the new settlers against the Natives was not only in Sherbro-Mende land but everywhere in the country where the Government assisted them to settle. In the North of the country, the situation became so much more serious that the Government in Freetown started to deploy the army against the Natives.

And this conflict spread over the entire country; the natives against foreign settlers, referred to as the 1898 war.

This war became really severe in Sherbro-Mende land. In the District of Imperri, the Resident Commissioner and his entire family were killed. Some members of the police force escaped the Poro Society attack, but the majority were killed and the barracks completely demolished. The American missionaries and foreigners that were married to native women were protected from the warriors. They were taken into the Poro Bush until the war ended.

The Aftermath and the Rebuild

The Government in Freetown mercilessly avenged the atrocities done on Sherbro-Mende land. Over one hundred of the suspects were condemned to death and killed and their leaders banished. When the war ended, surprisingly, the Government in Freetown called an American missionary, who was protected by Poro Society to become Chief in Imperri to facilitate reconciliation and help with the rebuilding. He accepted this position and decided to reside in Victoria, a developing commercial town in those days.

From here he was able to appease the Natives. He made effort to build schools and churches, and made more American missionaries to come and settle along the Sherbro River, that is known today as Bonthe District. This Missionary Chief stimulated commerce again in Sherbro-Mende land and improved the production and export of commodities from the area. Some of the descendants of this American, Poro Society-protected Chief, who knew their family history, have since shown up for every Paramount Chief election in the Imperri Chiefdom.

Regent Chiefs

Madam Hawa Kpanabom had known the Regent Chief for a long time. This was the second time he had been appointed Regent Chief in the Imperri Chiefdom. Regent Chiefs (Regents) are appointed by the Government to discharge the functions of a Paramount Chief in the case of death, or when the Chief is incapacitated. Regency is usually for a short period of time and involves the use of limited staff members. This was one such Regency.

Since the Chief had died, there was no Court Chairperson, neither was the mobile court functioning. The Regent had the court Chairperson selected, and had him reactivate the mobile court. There was no current report from the collection of weekly marker dues, either, so the case of market dues also became quickly organized and collectors were selected and put to work. The local tax collection was a very difficult task because of the high population of mine workers in the area. However, the Regent himself and the treasury clerk agreed to assume the responsibility of the tax collection, a tedious work, that required the handling of lots of chiefdom cash. The other areas from where the Chiefdom gets it funds are well documented; these are funds from the mining companies, considered surface rents, and funds from the mobile court.

The Regent maintains a small court made up of members of his choice. Some were Tribal Authorities, and others were Village Heads, whom he considered trustworthy and reliable. This Court meets every day of the week in the Chiefdom Headquarters. Members of this court receive and entertain, if possible, friendly visitors or Government Officials that visit the capital of the Chiefdom. Members of this court also have the right to intervene in disputes that can be easily solved. If they cannot easily solve a problem, they have the right to refer it to the regular court in the Chiefdom.

It is unusual to have extended Regency, although every Regent Chief would love to have his or her mandate extended. The longer they stay in this position the more money they will make. But the most important aspect of longer Regency is prestige and trust from both the Central Government and the Chiefdom people. The more the central government is satisfied with your performance, the longer they will keep you in a Regency position. However, the long Regency that existed in Imperri Chiefdom was partly due to the fact that the One Party civilian Central Government in Freetown was at the point of transferring power to the Military. They were ready for the Paramount Chief election in Imperri as soon as the power transfer in Freetown was completed.

Honouring the Ancestors

Mama Hawa was elected. Her first move was to feed the crowd and make food available in her compound for a week for those who wanted more food. While her jubilant supporters continued to dance, singing and praising her, she kept busy consulting with the Regent Chief. While she continued to pick the brain of the Regent, they agreed on the sacred transfer of the Chiefdom Power to the Chief that had been genuinely elected by the Government.

This event involves the officiation of Libation for the Chief elect. Libation of this kind requires special food and drinks prepared for the Ancestors. In the Imperri Chiefdom, this sacred ritual required the representatives of Poro Society, Bondo Society, Njayee Society and Humoi Society. In addition, some Tribal Authorities and Section Chiefs are required to be present. An effort was immediately made to get these people. When this audience was ready, Mama Hawa opened the meeting by greeting them, and thanking them for coming. She then asked the outgoing Regent Chief to speak.

The Regent Chief expressed his appreciation to Mama Hawa, then said, "This is your day, Mama." Then the Regent continued, "All those people we invited are here. Thank you very much for coming. You must all have an idea about why you are here today. We are here to give food and drinks to our Ancestors and to put Mama Hawa into their hands for their guidance and protection.

"You are all aware of our location along the Atlantic Coast and some of our history, both ancient and recent. Our coast was used as an anchorage for foreign merchant ships. Some of the merchants went along our tributaries to get fresh drinking water, others for trade in commodities, and still others to capture our young men and women for a trade in the New World. The spirit of our Ancestors remained connected to those individuals who were removed from our land. Our Ancestors see us everywhere we go, and they hear every word we say. Our entire spirit is connected to theirs.

"Oh, how much joy and happiness do we derive from praising and giving thanks to our Ancestors! We inherited fertile farm lands, where we grow our crops and reap good harvest. Although we have occasional disaster wherein our crops and villages are subjected to destruction by flood and wild animals, we still always express our gratitude and appreciation to our Ancestors who had established us in this Chiefdom, many, many years ago.

"In the years following the abolition of the slave trade, there was a large number of new settlers in our Chiefdom. They were assisted by the Government in Freetown. They were made to settle in economically viable areas, on fertile farm lands and palm fruit producing areas. These settlers were mostly businessmen and tradesmen. Some of them made deals with the land owners, and bought them out; others forced the land owners to vacate their properties, leaving them for the new settlers.

"A Resident Commissioner was then assigned and located at Kpangbama, where a police barracks was constructed. Around this same period, American missionaries moved into the Hinterland. They built churches and schools as they advanced further into the interior. But, unfortunately, both the Government in Freetown and the American missionaries were only interested in improving the lives of the new settlers. There was no interest in dealing with the primitive and fetishistic natives.

"During the war of 1898, the Commissioner, the police force and the new settlers suffered greatly. The Imperri Chiefdom became completely disorganized. The Government in Freetown selected an American missionary to become Chief of the Imperri Chiefdom. A missionary, who was a survivor of the war, accepted this position. He played a major role in the improvement of education in the Bonthe District as a whole, by building schools and churches in areas where they were needed. He helped to revive commerce along the Sherbro River and along the major tributaries that lead to major towns in the Bonthe District.

"The American missionary named Chief of Imperri Chiefdom also helped the natives and settlers reconcile by having their children to attend the same schools and churches. The Chieftaincy came back to the natives of Imperri as soon as the American missionary retired.

"Who would have imagined that Bonthe District would become a mining District?

For generations, the place was known for commodities and agricultural products. It was the space age that brought high demand for titanium, that brought the British Titanium Product Company, led by Doctor Joyce to prospect for titanium in the Imperri Chiefdom, and for bauxite in other parts of the Bonthe District. The presence of these minerals was so evident, in particular that of rutile in the Imperri Chiefdom that the processing plant was quickly constructed following the mining.

"Shipment of the final product was later arranged as the finished product accumulated. The Europeans eventually took over the mining and shipping of the bauxite while the Americans took over the mining of the titanium from the British Titanium Product Company.

"As the demand for the final product of the mining companies increased, managements in these companies did employ more workers to increase the production. The Senior staff Quarters, Intermediates, Junior, and the Security Men's Quarters were all running at full capacity in the companies. In addition, unskilled labour in the companies also considerably increased.

"The Imperri Chiefdom Administration had no provision to deal with such a population in the Mine Sites. However, in my capacity, serving in a second Regency position, I have the right to do changes acceptable to the Chiefdom. I did accept to collect the local tax with the help of the Treasury Clerk. This was indispensable, mainly because there was a large population and quite a bit of cash to handle for the Chiefdom. Equally, I restructured the mobile court, and allowed it to run with my selected Court Chairman. This has been quite satisfactory.

"This has been my second Regency. It has been long and demanding, but rewarding and honourable. We are gathered here in the presence of our Ancestors to feed them, and to pour Sacred Libation for them. We are here making an ardent appeal to our Ancestors to protect and guide Mama Hawa as she takes over the leadership and the administration of Imperri Chiefdom."

"Thank you all for coming," Mama Hawa responded, then continued, "I solemnly accept my responsibilities. Our Ancestors will protect and guide me."

There was no shortage of well-wishers among the Chiefdom people, the foreign and national mineworkers, and the neighbouring Chiefs. Most European and American Senior Staff members in the companies came in groups; some came singly to express their compliments to Mama Hawa. They came with various kinds of gifts: artwork, clothes, paintings, drinks, and money.

The general manager of the Rutile Mines and his business manager organized a supper in the Chief Compound. This was well received and highly appreciated by the Chief. Some mineworkers that were really anxious to have the Chief know them came with their complimentary gift to the Chief at the time when they were not expected. However, they, too, were welcomed and not turned away.

In Sherbro-Mende Land, well-wishing a newly elected Paramount Chief is a ritual that is performed according to the profession and social position of the individual in the Chiefdom. In this case, a hunter came with a whole deer that he had just killed, and presented it as a complimentary gift to the Chief. The immediate response was to have the hunter butcher the deer, leave some of the meat in the Chief's Compound, give some away and take the rest of the meat home.

Two other hunters also followed the deer hunter. The first one was an elephant hunter. He came with a valuable elephant tusk for Mama Hawa, which was highly appreciated, but, he also brought a complaint for the Chief. The mining in the Chiefdom had driven the elephants away.

The second hunter came with a gorgeous buffalo skin as a complimentary gift for the Chief, and had the same complaint as the elephant hunter. The mining activities in the Chiefdom has made the buffalo leave the area. The hunters had a genuine complaint to the Chief.

Expressing a complaint to a newly elected Chief is not the right time. When the trappers and the fishermen were ready to give complaint to the Chief, they would come to the Chief Compound.

The trapper came with a wild boar he had just caught, while the fishermen came with baskets of raw and dry fish. They were followed by those who came with chickens, goats, sheep, money and other valuables. It was all out of goodwill. The Chiefdom did not make any appeal for what was received.

General Chiefdom Meeting

While the well-wishers were being cordially received, a general Chiefdom meeting was scheduled for Village Heads, Town Chiefs, Section Chiefs, and Tribal Authorities to take place at the earliest possible time. The aim for this meeting was to help Mama Hawa to familiarize herself with current events in the Chiefdom and to get to know the people with whom she was going to work. This meeting brought to light the main problems the Chiefdom was facing.

The Village Heads informed the Chief that the Villages in the Chiefdom were going to completely disappear in a short time because there were neither young men nor young women in the Villages. They had all deserted the Villages. There were no men available to maintain the roads between villages in the Chiefdom, neither to harvest the high yielding coffee and cacao plantations. Many fertile farm lands in the villages were lying fallow.

The mine sites and the neighbouring towns were overcrowded. More than half of the population were not company workers. But the Chiefdom has no control over those on company premises. The companies have their security men that have the right to get rid of squatters on their property. The policemen on the other hand, in nice clean uniforms, are always in their station.

There are different groups of policemen at the mine sites. There are those in uniform that spend their day in the station. The company security men have their own uniforms, easily distinguishable from others. But there are two other groups of policemen, known as Internal Security Unit (I.S.U.) and Security Safety Division (S.S.D.). It is essential for the Chiefdom policemen to know the limit of their power among these security forces. The population in the mine sites and the neighbouring towns outnumber that of the entire Chiefdom. The Chiefdom has to consider maintaining a permanent court session in the area, with its Court Chairperson and clerks, independent of the Mobile Court. Of course, such a court would only handle cases that are within its control.

There were many things in the Chiefdom that Mama Hawa needed to know, but what had been mentioned in this first meeting was enough for her first day. There were other sources from which she could obtain accurate information about the Chiefdom. However, these types of meetings were indispensable for a new Paramount Chief.

Family

There is truly an immense joy in getting to the top of the Native Administration in one's Chiefdom. Mama Hawa had certainly, comfortably attained this pinnacle. All evidence indicated that she had the support of the entire Chiefdom.

As the hype of the election success started to wane, she quickly selected the people she needed to run the Chiefdom. It was then time to get to work. She took a trip to Bo Town. Her destination was Number 14 Ngaru Road, the home of Mi Maseray, a wealthy distant aunt who had brought her up as a young girl. Mi Maseray and her children had since passed away, but her grandchildren and great-grandchildren still lived in that same home. But they had never heard about their distant relatives in the Imperri Chiefdom, and that the daughter of the Chief in that Chiefdom had been brought up by their great-grandmother in their house. Mama Hawa entered the house, sat down, told her story to Mi Maseray's grandchildren, gave them a gift, then left.

Next, she went directly to Number 1 Mission Road, the compound of Mama Yarkai's children. Mama Yarkai was a relative of late P.C. Kpanabom of Imperri Chiefdom, and she, with Mi Maseray, took care of Mama Hawa when she was a young girl of school age. When she arrived, one of Mama Yarkai's children recognized her, and she came and embraced her, expressing compliments to her, and they exchanged gifts. The mission of this day trip to Bo Town was to visit with distant relatives, formally inform them about her achievement and express her appreciation for the role they had played in her life.

On her return home, Mama Hawa planned to return all the visits she had received from her neighbours, which included Banta Gbangbatok, Banta Mokle and Mattru Jong.

The Chief in Mattru Jong was then Sam Goba. He and his Chiefdom Speaker, Alhaji Lowece, had made a good contribution during the election and also a large donation after the election. The visit to Mattru Jong was very cordial. There was a lot of food and drink shared, followed by exchange of gifts.

A few days after visiting Sam Goba, Mama Hawa went on to visit Chief Sam Margai in Gangbatoke. A dancing group welcomed her. They were entertained for the whole day by drumming, singing, and dancing all day. There was more food and drink, and eventually the Chiefs exchanged gifts at the end.

It was more than a week before Mama Hawa decided to go to Mokle to visit Chief Edward Jombla. He had arranged for Bondo Devil dancing and drummers as a welcome. Mama Hawa danced with the Bondo Devil around the town. There was again lots of food and drink. This was another day trip. By the time Mama Hawa was ready to leave, most of those who were drumming, singing, and dancing were all drunk. It was surely a fun day.

These visits did not end with the visit to friendly Paramount Chiefs. Mama Hawa wanted to visit with one northern province Chief. Chief Dura of Binkolo was the longest serving Paramount Chief in the country. Since she was a newly elected Chief, she needed the advice of some of the long-serving Chiefs. She had spent some time learning about what Chief Dura would like to receive as a gift, and then collected the items she needed for her visit. The plan for the visit was to arrive at Binkolo early in the morning and spend the whole day there.

On the day of their departure, Mama Hawa was informed that Chief Dura woke late every day. Once he was out of bed, he would go for a swim in the river in his area before he getting ready to receive visitors. That meant that he would be ready to receive visitors around noon every day. This did not change Mama Hawa's time of departure. She decided to add another visit to her agenda.

She departed early according to plan, and made a surprise visit to Chief Kandeh Saiwoh in Kalangba, a close family friend, who had worked as a policeman before he was crowned Paramount Chief. The distance between Kalangba and Binkolo is only twenty miles. Mama Hawa made it to Binkolo around noon to visit with Chief Dura.

He was a small man, not quite five feet tall, but wearing an oversize native gown. He was surrounded by his Tribal Authorities. Each of these men came to shake hands with Mama Hawa. Apart from Chief Dura, all these men needed an interpreter to talk to Mama Hawa. They spoke neither Creole nor Mende. However, they appeared to be pleased with the visit. The food and drinks that Mama Hawa brought were served. While everyone was enjoying the food, Mama Hawa sat listening to what Chief Dura had to say to her. When she finished consulting with Chief Dura, it was time to go home.

Chapter 2: Making the Chief

The Compound

The Compound of Paramount Chief Kpanabom was a rectangular shape, with two gates, both of them located at the center of the rectangular wall. The North gate, with a façade extending north, had rooms and apartments on both sides, with kitchens on both extremes. The South Gate, with façade facing inward, north, also had rooms and apartments on both sides.

There were series of buildings inside the Compound. The one that stood out most of all was the one where the Chief slept. It was a small house, painted white, with a large front door opening into a long verandah, and a back door opening into the washroom. In the middle of the Compound was an all-purpose building, known as the small court, where visitors were received, place where food was served to the public, and where family court matters were held. Near the small court building, was a board house, built on a concrete slab, that served as a guest house, and also as a house where valuables of the family and gifts were kept.

Between Mi Mojama's house and her kitchen and Mi Sahn's house and her kitchen was the apartment and the workshop of the goldsmith. Mi Mojama was the youngest in the family of three; two females and one male. Mi Njahawah, the eldest, the mother of Mi Ndaneh was to have become Paramount Chief in Imperri Chiefdom, but she gave it up for her younger brother, Kpanabom. Mi Njahawah preferred to continue to be the head of Njayei in Mbeleh Town. Mi Mojama had two sons, George Kpewoh and Alfred Kpanabom. She was the brain in her brothers' compound; she managed their wealth and made major family decisions. Mi Sahn was the cleverest and the most dependable of the many women in Chief Kpanabom's Compound. Her father was a

Paramount Chief. She was brought up in the chief's compound, and she was quite familiar with the routine.

In addition to Mi Mojama's kitchen and Mi Sahn's kitchen, there was a third kitchen in the Compound, referred to as the general kitchen. In this kitchen, there was always a pot boiling. Although Mi Sahn provided enough food to be cooked to feed everyone in the Compound, there were always those busy cooking their food privately. The food production, which was centered in Gbonjeima was in the hands of Mi Mojama and Mi Sahn the most powerful women in the Chief Compound. It was their responsibility to keep Chief Kpanabom (Leleeh) informed about the quantity of food they had in stock at all times, and how much needed to be produced in the following year. The food management for chiefs that had a large following was not easy. They always had to have enough food to feed their dependents and give some away to friends and relatives. To be able to do this, the farms have to be made bigger and more productive each year. Fortunately, the entire chiefdom was willing to help during the farming season.

This was the Compound in which Bio Hawa was born to Mi Kemah and Chief Kpanabom (Leleeh). At a very early age, Mi Mojama took care of this child even when her mother was not busy. She assumed the responsibility to feed her and attend to her as if she were the real mother. Her brother Leleeh used to tease her: "You made boys only. You never made any girls. Now you have got one. Take good care of her." Boi Hawa slept in Mi Mojama's house. On a busy day, she would carry Boi Hawa on her back. She cooked regularly for her brother, and that's the food Boi Hawa and her father ate.

Time goes fast, and it seemed the children grew even faster. Boi was far from school age, but she was beginning to understand how much attention and care she was receiving in her father's compound. One day, Mi Mojama told her that she was going to take her to Bo Town and buy new dresses, shoes, and head-ties, and that she was preparing for that trip. Meanwhile, Boi Hawa had nothing else to talk about except her new clothes and shoes she would get in Bo Town. Mi Mojama got the food required and the carries ready for the trip. The carries accompanied Mi Mojama and Boi Hawa to Mattru Jong. From there, a vehicle took them to Number 14 Ngaru Road in Bo Town. There was no time lost in buying Boi Hawa's beautiful dresses and shoes. She liked them so much she spent the whole day in front of her mirror admiring them.

Mi Maseray made Boi comfortable in this new place. Things were quite different from that of her father's compound, but from the time she arrived, she had enjoyed playing and eating together with the grandchildren in the house. This was a good sign that she was accepted to stay, although she had not yet been informed that by bringing her to Mi Maseray in Bo Town, it was intended for her to stay there permanently and attend school. She was eventually told when Mi Mojama returned home without saying goodbye to her. It had been a trick. Everybody thought that Boi Hawa would not leave Leleeh's Compound for anywhere else. But when she was brought to Mi Maseray by trick, and she found the conditions there were suitable, she happily accepted to stay there. And there she was able to acquire most of the knowledge she needed to become Paramount Chief of Imperri Chiefdom.

Mi Maseray was a wealthy widow who traced her ancestors from Mbeleh Town and was related to the Kpanabom family. Her children often came to Imperri during the farming season, grew their crop in Gbonjeima and then returned to Bo Town after the harvest. She was happy to have Boi Hawa in her household. She always had the conviction that she was making one of the future Paramount Chiefs of Imperri.

Schooling

Boi Hawa was a fast learner. Even before she was of school age, she wore her school uniform and went to school regularly with the older children in the house. As young as she was, she learned to make up her bed each morning, helped the older children with the cleaning of the yard, and would also collect water from the stream daily for the house. Under the guidance of Mi Maseray, and by observing and following what the older children in the house were doing, Boi Hawa picked up basic housekeeping skills at an early age.

There is a saying that "school days are the best", but early school days, or the beginning of any project is not easy. Early school days were not easy for Boi Hawa. There were no friends. It was all ABCD, 1234, the black board, and the teacher in a white-white. There were no jokes, no playing, just the actual magistral type of instruction. Many children would come to this school for just a few weeks, get turned off, and never came back, but Boi Hawa continued to go to school because it was nearer 14 Ngaru Road. And, if she did not go to the school, she would not have had anything to do at home. Eventually, she got to meet other children who had gone to that school at different time periods. She changed her time to match that of her newfound friends. This made the school more attractive to them, even to those who had left the school. They saw school as a place to learn and to play.

During the periodic gathering of Paramount Chiefs of Sierra Leone in Bo Town, Leleeh used to stay with Mama Yarkai in Chief Joe Boim's Compound. They traced their ancestors from Sherbro-Mende land, more precisely, from Imperri Chiefdom. Through marriage and business ventures they became Chiefs of the Kakowah Chiefdom. Their children had always been taught the story of their ancestors.

While Leleeh was in Bo Town for the Paramount Chief Assembly, he introduced Boi Hawa to Mama Yarkai. This was the time when Mama Yarkai was contesting the Chieftaincy for the Kakowah Chiefdom against J.B. Hotaguan. From that time, Mama Yarkai frequently asked Boi Hawa to accompany her to Chiefdom meetings, to carry her chair. When the election finished, in which the Boima Family lost, Mama Yarkai wanted Boi Hawa to come and stay with her in her compound. But this was impossible because she had to continue with her school on Ngaru Road. However, she regularly visited Mama Yarkai, helped her with cleaning and carrying water for her when required.

It was through these regular visits to Mama Yarkai that she was able to meet Mama Yarkai's grandchildren—Amara Fofana's daughter, Aminata Fofana, and Umu's son, Ayor Johnson. Boi Hawa was older than these children and was able to render more help when Mama Yarkai required. The friendship that developed between the three of them opened a wider scope for Boi Hawa in Bo Town. Although the three of them attended different schools, they were able to meet and play regularly in Mama Yarkai's Compound, or at Number 1 Mission Road, where the parents of Aminata and Ayor lived; the Compound of Mama Yarkai's children.

As she grew older, Boi Hawa had no problem doing her school work, while at the same time attending to housekeeping duties, highly required for a growing girl as insisted upon by Mi Maseray. When Mama Yarkai needed some help, she would send Aminata to come and get her. In those days, Aminata was attending Q.R.S. Catholic School for Girls which was not far away from 14 Ngaru Road. Aminata and Boi Hawa usually arranged firewood collection for Mama Yarkai as well as for Mi Maseray. The requirement for firewood for these people, or really everywhere in Bo Town, was considered an urgent matter during the Fast Month. Consequently, these young girls started firewood collection and stock piling ahead of the Fast Month in order to avoid the unnecessary rush during the Fast Month.

At this stage in her life, Boi Hawa had learned to assume complete housekeeping for Mi Maseray, as well as assist Mama Yarkai with hers. These were reputable Muslim homes where the owners had always provided food for other Muslims during the Month of Ramadan. Boi Hawa was quite familiar with the type of food, the way it was prepared and served to the fasting Muslims in the evening, when they ended the fast, and early in the morning when the fasting started. Those fasting would always appreciate freshly cooked food that was expected to stay longer in the stomach. Those responsible for the cooking and the serving of that food had to decide on having the cooking done early in the morning, every day for the entire Month of Ramadan. Both Mi Maseray and Mama Yarkai always had their helpers available for this job. That was where Boi Hawa was highly appreciated by all of those who benefited from her willingness to serve at all times.

Every year, Boi Hawa received gifts of new dresses from both Mi Maseray and Mama Yarkai at the end of Muslim month of fasting the "Eid Ul-Fitre". Ramadan in Bo Town, in those days, ended with Muslim public prayers in public parks or in open fields, depending on the area of town. Following the prayers in the open air, communal meals are served to the public regardless of religious conviction. The festivities will continue for a day or two singing religious songs praising the Prophet Mohammed. Boi Hawa was introduced to both Christianity as well Islam in her youth. In school, it was Christianity, reading the Bible. Most of the schools in Bo Town in those days had been built by missionaries who taught their pupils to read the Bible and become Christians. In both Mi Maseray and Mama Yarkai's households, Boi Hawa was completely immersed in Islam, though she was never taught the Koran. But she learned to assist people to pursue their Islamic activities.

Meetings & Celebrations

Boi Hawa bore witness to Bo Town's fast growth in her youth. She was there when the first Cinema Hall was built on Kissy Town Road. She and her best friend Aminata Fofana spent a good number of their Sunday Afternoons watching Cowboy films there.

Bo Town became the venue of all the major events in the Protectorate of Sierra Leone. Some of the most important that brought people from every part of the country included: the Empire Day Celebration, the Coronation Day Celebration, Paramount Chief Meetings, Agricultural Shows, and the Colony and protectorate sporting events. In the Protectorate, the Queen Elizabeth II's Coronation Day Celebration and the Empire Day Celebration were combined into one event. All the students in the

Protectorate came to Bo Town for a week, where they competed in group sports and individual activities.

The Celebration always ended with a match-pass on the streets in Bo Town. Boi Hawa liked this event the best out of all others. On the day of the match-pass, she would get into her school uniform early in the morning and then run to their school from where the matching started. All the participating schools would make their way to the Coronation Ground, where they were addressed by the Commissioner of the Crown, then gifts from the Queen of England were distributed to all the students. From the Coronation Ground, the students marched in the streets of Bo Town in their colourful school uniforms. This was one of the best annual entertainment events in Bo Town. Parents and guardians would line the streets to watch their children matching, all of them dressed up in their beautiful, colourful school uniforms.

The Empire Day Celebrations were well organized and made suitable for the youth. The games, cricket and football [soccer] matches were organized for professional players. There were no games organized for juniors and intermediate youths; if there were any, they must have been in the Colony in Freetown.

The Annual Agricultural Shows were events organized mainly for adults, professionals and businessmen. Although the show brought lots of people to Bo Town, there were no programs for the youth, except to render domestic help to homes where the participants stayed. Of course, most of the produce, lifestock, and other items usually brought for the show, got sold before the show ended.

Boi Hawa's favourite of the events in Bo Town organized by the Central Government was that of the periodic meetings of Paramount Chiefs. Her father Leleeh regularly attended these meetings. It was a point of duty for him to get to Bo Town with his drummers and dancing group two days before the actual meeting. His permanent residence was Mama Yarkai's Compound.

Mama Yarkai and her children, at Number 1 Mission Road regularly provided accommodation for two Paramount Chiefs during their meetings in Bo Town, Chief Leleeh and Chief Gulama. From the moment of his arrival in Bo Town, Leleeh would immediately give out the gifts he had for both Mi Maseray and Mama Yarkai. He also gave gifts to other friendly Paramount Chiefs. The Chiefs did try to maintain cordial relationships among themselves. The main aim of the Central Government in bringing them together periodically was to enforce this kind of friendly relationship. They provided generous sustenance to all households that provided accommodation for

Paramount Chiefs during the Assembly.

Paramount Chiefs came to these meetings with their Dancing Groups, drummers and singers. A good number of them were really skillful, and they were able to raise funds by playing at the different households where Chiefs were accommodated. Salia Koroma, a famous accordionist of Paramount Chief Francis Kposowa, took advantage of this, and he was quite successful. He was quite motivated. In each known Paramount Chief meeting he was always able to visit each of them and play his accordion to entertain them.

Each time Salia Koroma came to Mama Yarkai's Compound to play for both Leleeh and Chief Gulama, Boi Hawa and her friends would dance to his music. All the meetings of the Paramount Chiefs were closed door meetings, but the final meetings usually took place at the Coronation Ground, where the Chiefs' dancing groups performed, and then the Commissioner of Queen Elizabeth II would address all those gathered for the close.

Chief Leleeh stayed longer in Bo Town than usual. He had arrived two days earlier. What was in the baskets of gifts he brought for his relatives in Bo Town? Farm produce, bags of rice, fresh fish, dried fish, salted and fried fish. The fish was all ocean fish, which was not easy to get in Bo Town because it's located so far away from the ocean.

Boi Hawa took advantage of her father's stay to get familiar with his dancing group. She had them frequently play for her and her friends to dance. They followed Salia Koroma as he went from one household to another to play and entertain Chiefs in order to solicit funds.

They were with him at Number 1 Mission Road where he played for Chief Gulama and his entourage. From Chief Gulama's, Salia Koroma went to Mama Yarkai's Compound to play for Chief Leleeh. On his arrival, Chief gave him some cash. He immediately started to sing and play his accordion. Boi Hawa and her friends, and Leleeh's group joined in the dancing. The merriment continued till late at night, even after Salia Koroma had left.

Bio Hawa had never witnessed the closing ceremony of the Paramount Chief's Meetings. Now that she was old enough to take part in such an event, she went with her father and his dancing group to the Coronation Ground. This was a cultural event, wherein all the Chiefs present had their groups sing, drum, and dance for the public. The performances were not meant to be a competition. There was no deciding which

Chief had the best singers, drummers, or dancers. The only objective was for the Paramount Chiefs of the Protectorate to entertain the public of Bo Town. The last activity of the event was an address from the Commissioner of the Queen of England.

During this Assembly of Paramount Chiefs in Bo Town, Leleeh was able to see how enlightened his daughter had become. Mama Yarkai and Mi Maseray were highly impressed by her behaviour and they spoke kindly of her to her father. He was absolutely amused watching his daughter and her friends dancing to Salia Koroma's accordion music. He was equally impressed by the way his daughter associated herself with members of his dancing group, and how she helped them go about their private business while in Bo Town, especially those who were in Bo Town for the first time. The silly little girl he had known in Leleeh's Compound in Kpangbama some years ago had seen the light of Bo Town. She had grown.

Chapter 3: Secret Bondo Society

Coming Home

Mi Maseray took Boi Hawa to a tailor she had known for many years on Kissy Town Road, Bo Town. She had all the materials she had requested; some yards of cotton, silk, and velvet for dresses to be made for her. Boi Hawa could not understand why such lavish clothing had been selected for her.

When the dresses were ready, Mi Maseray took her to the Bata Shoe Store to buy her some pairs of shoes. They didn't look at jewelry such as necklaces, bracelets or bangles. A resident goldsmith in Leleeh's Compound could provide these items.

Events in Boi Hawa's life had come to her through her "lucky star". A day before her departure to Kpangbama, Mi Maseray finally declared that it was time for Boi Hawa to go home to be initiated into the Bondo Society.

Boi Hawa did not know where Kpangbama, the place of her birth, was. Although, when she was growing up in Bo Town, she was taught that she was the daughter of a Sherbro-Mende Chief, Paramount Chief Kpanabom (Leleeh) of Imperri Chiefdom, Bonthe District. She had met and spent some time with her father during his visit to Bo Town for Government Affairs. But she had never been to her place of birth since she was sent to live with relatives in Bo Town. She had a faint memory of Mi Mojama, who carried her on her back, brought her to Number 14 Ngaru Road, in Bo Town, left her there with Mi Maseray, then returned home without saying goodbye to her. She also had a faint memory of Mi Sahn who took care of her all day and fed her when she was hungry. She remembered her mother, Mi Kemah, who spent her entire day in the general kitchen, cooking to feed the hungry in the Chief Compound.

The titanium and the bauxite mining companies came to the Bonthe and

Moyamba Districts in a rush. They constructed the motor road from Moyamba Junction to Senehun, Jong Chiefdom with feeder roads, connecting Keiga, Yargoi, Victoria, Momaligue and Nitti Habour. British Titanium Product (B.T.P.), had established their headquarters at Kpangbama, while that of the SIEROMCO, the bauxite company, was established at Gbangbatok (Mokanji).

The products generated by these two companies were in high demand during the competition to build space ships to go to the moon by the Western powers. They were involved in prospecting, mining and shipping their products. They had an arrangement with the government through the Minister of Mines, Lands and Labour (Hon. Siaka Stevens), in Milton Margai's government, in those days, to reside in Mattru Jung, for a given period of time, to ensure quick consultations. Hon. Siaka Stevens resided in Abraham Tucker's house, which faced the old market, near Abu Jallor's shop. The companies picked him up every day by vehicle to the Mining Sites, or by speed boat to the shipping areas. This process continued until there was a slowdown in frequent government consultations.

There were four chiefdoms under the influence of these moving mining companies, known as Mining Area Chiefdoms: Imperri, Banta Gbangbatok, Banta Mokele, and Mano Darse. There were more American and European mine workers in these Chiefdoms than anywhere else in West Africa. Other professionals, mine workers, and school leavers came to the area for employment. Lots of them were employed, but there were a lot more looking for work. Those who were working and had nowhere to stay and those who had no work and no food all took refuge in the Chief Compound.

This was exactly the situation when the chiefdom vehicle arrived home from Bo Town with Boi Hawa.

"What a stranger!" greeted Mi Mojama.

What were her capabilities to find solutions for the current problems in the Chief Compound? She had been away from home since she was a very young child. But she certainly had had the full apprenticeship training from Mi Maseray and Mama Yarkai to become Paramount Chief of Imperri. Although she had not been initiated into the Secret Bondo Society yet, she did not hesitate to make bold decisions in the Chief Compound, because she knew her father would not reject them.

She immediately decided to relieve the older people in the Compound of their tedious duties. She reduced the three kitchens in the Compound, that had existed for decades, to one general kitchen, of which she took charge. Mi Mojama's and Mi Sahn's kitchens, were then to be used only for food storage for home consumption or food intended to go out as gifts.

Boi Hawa was able to make the general kitchen cook enough food so that the employed mine workers and unemployed personnel who regularly came to the Compound for food would get at least a plate of rice a day.

Around the same time, B.T.P. decided to feed their workers. There was no place in the Chiefdom, and in particular, in the Town of Kpangbama, where a person with lots money could easily get food to buy. In those days, one had to go along the cost, in places where the merchants were established—Victoria, Kpangbaia or Mattru Jong—to get food to buy. As a result, the Company also decided to provide food for those people who were looking for work and had the chance of getting employed. They came to the Chief Compound to see if it was possible to buy enough food from them regularly to feed their workers. They got some food, because they were pressed, but Leleeh refused to continue to sell food to them.

Boi Hawa had the all-purpose small court building in the middle of the Compound cleaned out. The old benches and hammocks were removed and replaced with new ones. The family valuables and luxury items that were kept in the Board House were removed and sent to be kept in Mi Mojama's house, and she occupied the Board House. The goldsmith of the Compound had disappeared a while ago. Nobody in the Compound knew his whereabouts. He did not leave any account of the Chiefdom Valuables that were under his control. Some jewelry and gold dust were found in his workshop. These items were removed and stored in Leleeh's House.

Since the B.T.P. was having difficulties getting two meals a day for its employees, the Chief Compound had the pressure to give at least a plate of rice to those who regularly came for food. Consequently, Boi Hawa had to go to Gbonjeima to arrange for more rice and farm produce to be transferred to the Compound because she had more people to feed. Food was not available to be sold, but there was always enough to eat and share in Leleeh's Compound.

It was indispensable that B.T.P. hastily looked for food for the large population of people that had drowned the Chiefdom. They were able to quickly solve the food problem, providing two meals for all their employees, and all those who showed up for food were served. The Company also assisted local merchants with the provisioning. This arrangement did reduce the pressure on the Chief Compound in the feeding of outsiders.

Initiation Day

The time for the initiation into the Secret Bondo Society came, but Boi Hawa had disappeared.

Don't ask me where the Secret Bondo Society bush and house were and what happened there. It is a secret. A man is not supposed to know. That is the woman's world.

One thing I got to know for sure was that all the changes Boi Hawa made in her father's Compound when she returned from Bo Town remained intact while she was gone. The Compound dwellers and those who came to visit, for court matters, or for their daily food all appreciated the changes. One might have imagined that in the absence of Boi Hawa, Mi Mojama and Mi Sahn would have returned to the comforts of their individual kitchens they had always had in Leleeh's Compound. On the contrary, they did not because Boi Hawa had trained her helpers in the single kitchen to always clean the area well, to cook as early as possible during the day for everyone, and to serve the food as efficiently as she herself did serve.

A fundamental practice in Sherbro-Menda Land is to initiate all their young girls into the Secret Bondo Society before they get married or before they pursue a career. There are variants in the rituals involved, depending on the individual initiators, and the place and the time of the initiation. In the case of Boi Hawa and her colleagues, when they went for the initiation, they had to completely avoid areas where a man (male) could see them for two weeks. This is the period of no contact with men.

The second stage, which took another two weeks, involved them getting up very early every morning, collecting water from the river, coming back to the Bondo House, and practicing singing and dancing the Bondo Dance.

The third stage comprised of soliciting funds for the Society by going to sing and dance in different places and asking for money. When it was time for them to go out and sing and dance and solicit funds, their first show was in Victoria, a town along the coast, where there were many foreign Merchants and wealthy traders. Their second show was at Kpangbama, in Leleeh's Compound. It was a grand show for the Bondo Society. It was crowded by the mine workers, who generously contributed to the show. The Society must have surely collected a good sum of money from this show. The Society did continue to organize singing and dancing shows for their initiates in areas populated with mine workers. The Bondo Society came back to Victoria for their final show and to thank the merchants there for their generous contribution to their fundraising show.

Towards the final stages of the initiation into the Secret Bondo Society, the initiates are allowed to leave the Bondo House and go home for the whole day, to help their parents and relatives, and to also prepare for their graduation day. This was the time they bought new dresses and shoes. But they had to go back to the Bondo House and sleep there daily. Boi Hawa regularly came home with her colleagues. Sometimes, as soon as they got into the Compound, Mi Mojama would take them to Gbonjeima to help bring some food to the Compound in Kpangbama, and sometimes she came alone and assumed her responsibilities in her father's Compound. All the clothes she needed for this occasion were bought by Mi Maseray in Bo Town before coming home. Of course, her colleagues also had to get their clothes and shows ready before the final day.

On the graduation day from the Secret Bondo Society, the initiates wear their new dresses and new shoes, and they march together with their initiators to Leleeh's Compound where a place was prepared and reserved for them. The initiates stayed together in the Compound for three days. On the fourth day, they were all gone. Their parents and their fiancées came for them. Boi Hawa was the only initiate that remained in her father's Compound. Already a beautiful and tall young woman, the Secret Bondo Society initiation made her more confident of her womanhood, and what she was capable of doing as a woman. She proved to be a perfect product of a girl made into a woman by Secret Bondo Society. She continued to wear her new dresses and shoes, interchangeably—blue velvet, white silk, and cotton materials. She never dropped her jewelry any day. She did carry her gold earrings, necklaces, bracelet and bangles. Nevertheless, she attended to all the duties her father required her to do in the Compound.

Tradition Versus Progress

There was always opposition and criticism on the way girls were initiated in to the Secret Bondo Society in Imperri Chiefdom, particularly in Kpangbama, even when the daughter of the Paramount Chief was involved as an initiate. The opponents argue on different aspects of the initiation. Their arguments were related to the very fundamentals of the initiation—training of the initiates, the time involved, and the fundraising activities.

They thought that concealing the young women from men for only two weeks was not good enough, and that four weeks of concealment or longer was more appropriate. The concealment should be done the same way as it was done in olden days, so that the initiators would have adequate time to teach their subjects childbearing activities, childcare, nutrition and required cleanliness in their future homes, while, at the same time, attending to the home and the husband. They argued that the life skills the young women learn in the Secret Bondo Society Bush could not be acquired anywhere else, except in that Bush. Therefore, the initiation should not be done in a rush.

The initiates should learn proper gardening skills, fishing skills, so that they would be able to adequately take care of themselves, their children, and their homes. They also insisted that all fundraising activities of the Society be made longer. Assuming that the more the initiates made a show of soliciting for funds, the more funds they would likely raise for the Society and the community as a whole.

The critics and the opposers of the way the young women were initiated into the Secret Bondo Society expressed their desire of doing things in the old way. The ancient way of initiating the young women into the Secret Bondo Society was considered detrimental, unhealthy, and antisocial. Therefore, Public Health officials, sociologists, and medical officers conducted a study into this ancient practice to find a way to improve on it; retaining its social importance, while improving the general hygiene and health of the participants. This study was done under the supervision of Dr. Margai, while he was the Medical Officer of the Bonthe District, resident in Bonthe.

Without making drastic changes to the ancient practices, they came out with a variant that the initiators should have a Public Health certification, and always carry a First-Aid box in both the Bondo House and Bush, and that they should periodically report to the Medical Officer the number of young women they have initiated. The initiating groups were also required to inform their Paramount Chiefs and Public Health Officer in their area about their intentions and performances. This variance to the Secret Bondo Society was called "Margai Jandeh or Margai Sandai", a descriptive Sherbro-Mende expression referring to Dr. Margai's addition to the Secret Bondo Society initiation. The initiation of Boi Hawa and her colleagues was quite in compliance with "Margai Jandeh".

Matchmaking & Goat Heads

These were times of intense mining activities in both Banta Gbangbatok Chiefdom and Imperri Chiefdom. The British Titanium Product company was expanding the three shipping points they had been using—Victoria, Momaligue, and Nitti. At the same time, they were expanding their Headquarters at Kpangbama, and bringing more American and European employees. The Government in Freetown did appreciate what the miners were doing. And since this area was the home of the Prime Minister, Dr. Margai, he and his ministers did frequently come to the area to facilitate the operations of the miners. When Dr. Margai was at Kpangbama, his office was in Leleeh's Compound. There he consulted with Dr. Joyce, the Manager of B.T.P., and the Manager for the Bauxite Mining Company in Gbagbatok about the problems they were having with the landowners. They did not have to go to Freetown to have their prospecting, shipping and mining problems solved; the government officials came to them to help solve their problems.

When Dr. Margai was at Kpangbama, he was used to spending long hours in his office, in Leleeh's Compound, interceding between the miners and the landowners. The mining companies were afraid of any obstacle that would delay their operations. Since they learned that their operation was in the Prime Minister's home, they made it a point of duty to bring him home, whenever possible. And when the Prime Minister was present, they were flexible in their deals, and eager to have the Prime Minister on their side.

Dr. Margai always wanted his food to be taken to the Guest House where he stayed. This was ideal for Mi Sahn who had always retained the position to serve higher level visitors and family members. Serving Dr. Margai in the Guest House gave Mi Sahn the opportunity to be able to talk to him while she was serving him. Daughter of a Paramount Chief, brought up in a Chief Compound when she was young, and exposed to businessmen and Colonial Officers at her adult age, she was quite manipulative in her way of life. She was able to convince Dr. Margai, the Prime Minister, a middle-aged man, to take his uncle's daughter, a young Secret Bondo Society girl, that had not known any man, as his wife. Dr. Margai accepted.

That same day, when Mi Sahn was taking Dr. Margai's food to the Guest House she had Boi Hawa come with her. When they got to the Guest House, Up the Hill at Kpangbama, there was no introduction. It was love at "first sight". The next day, when Dr. Margai came down the Hill and went to the Compound, he had Boi Hawa called to the small Court building in the middle of the Compound, where Leleeh was sitting, and he held Boi Hawa's hand and said, "Uncle, this is my goat head" (Sherbro-Mende riddle, translated into English). When you take your uncle's daughter as your wife, you are claiming free goat head from him. Leleeh just turned his head to them, as a sign of recognition, and smiled.

Mi Sahn was successful in matchmaking Boi Hawa and Dr. Margai. But there was still some doubt in Leleeh's Compound and among some family members as to whether Boi Hawa, young as she was, would stay longer with Dr. Margai as her husband. Leleeh shared this same doubt because he was aware that Dr. Margai had gotten married and had two daughters when he was in medical school in England. But his English wife and daughters never followed him to Sierra Leone. Leleeh was confident that Dr. Margai was quite capable of managing his own affairs.

However, his doubt about this relationship had more to do with his daughter, although she was lined up to become Paramount Chief of the Imperri Chiefdom, she was heading into a questionable relationship. Mi Mojama and Mi Sahn were instructed to go to Gbonjeima to get some bags of rice, some farm produce, and two goats for Boi Hawa to take to Freetown. Dr. Margai was supposed to finish his engagements with the miners and return to Freetown immediately. The arrangement was that when he arrived in Freetown, a vehicle would be dispatched to come to Kpangbama to collect Boi Hawa. The next day, the vehicle arrived in the Chief Compound. Mi Mojama and Mi Sahn were not ready yet with the items they wanted Boi Hawa to take with her. After two days of waiting, Boi Hawa and Mi Sahn arrived at the Lodge, the Prime Minister's Residence, Hills Station, Freetown.

The psychological battle that was raging between four powerful women was finally over. This battle was essentially to be able to have control over Boi Hawa's initiation into the Secret Bondo Society and to influence her to marry a man of their choice—Mi Maseray and Mama Yarkai in Bo Town, on one side, and Mi Mojama and Mi Sahn in Kpangbama, in Leleeh's Compound, on the other.

Two years prior to Leleeh having had Boi Hawa come to Kpangbama for her initiation, Mi Maseray and Mama Yarkai were constantly sending messages to Leleeh, to inform him that they were ready for Boi Hawa's initiation into the Secret Bondo Society and make her pursue a career in Bo Town or marry a man of their choice. But their ideas were not acceptable to either Mi Mojama and Mi Sahn nor to Leleeh himself. Finally, Leleeh made Boi Hawa come to Kpangbama for her initiation. After that, Mi Sahn made Dr. Margai to take Boi Hawa as his wife.

It was not unusual for elderly women in Sherbro-Mende culture to try to take control over young women during their initiation into the Secret Bondo Society, and eventually control them, or pressure them to marry a man of their choice. If the marriage worked well, that is with good offspring, the matchmaker would benefit the most, or would be more satisfied with her performance. Leleeh made his successful relatives in Bo Town raise his daughter in an enlightened environment, so that she would be able to head family responsibilities in the future. And surely, they had been successful in doing this. But he was unwilling to allow the relatives to take complete control over his daughter's life. He considered that future leaders in the Chiefdom should be exposed to various changes in life, like the one the Chiefdom was facing, and it was becoming uncontrollable.

Suddenly, two mining companies moved into the area. The titanium mining company selected Kpangbama as their headquarters, while the bauxite company selected Gbangbatok as theirs. They constructed motor roads across the Chiefdoms, and to all the sea ports that were easily accessible. While they were prospecting and shipping the samples out, at the same time they were mining and shipping both titanium and bauxite processed products from different ports along the Sherbro River. Such intense mining activities flocked the area with employed and unemployed mineworkers, and also school leavers, looking for work.

This was a new event in the Chiefdom. There was no housing for the miners, and no food to feed them. The majority of those looking for work, especially the young school leavers flocked into the Chief Compound both for food and lodging. Those responsible for food and housing in the Chiefdoms had never had such a situation, and they did not know what to do. Fortunately, this was the exact time when Boi Hawa returned from Bo Town. She assumed the responsibility of quickly reorganizing the Compound, starting to cook for everyone and serving at least a plate of rice to those who came to the Compound for food.

Chapter 4: The Three Sisters

Managing Food

The Chief Compound, in colonial days, was the place where everyone went for information, food and lodging in a Chiefdom. Leleeh's Compound was full of his relatives, his many wives, and workers. The Chiefdom did most of his farm work. They did the planting, the weeding and, at harvesting time, they harvested that portion of the crop that was good enough for the Chief to keep in storage and give some away to other relatives, the poor, or religious groups. The remaining crop in the field was for the many wives to harvest, process and sell, or process and keep. Whatever quantity of food the women were able to harvest from the farm was theirs. But in Leleeh's farming area, the cash crops—coffee, cacao, palm produce, kola nuts, and all the tropical fruit—were harvested, processed by his relatives and sold.

During the farming season, when these people had to work side by side, there was usually lots of interaction among them. But after the harvest, these people absolutely kept to themselves in their daily activities. This kind of behaviour had been the cause of petty jealousy developing among them in Leleeh's Compound. This made it really difficult to assist the large group of miners who were looking for help in the Chief Compound.

Leleeh made Boi Hawa come home to be initiated into the Secret Bondo Society, after she had had a good training in the hands of Mi Maseray and Mama Yarkai, and education in Bo Town.

On her arrival, she noticed that Kpangbama had been the Titanium Mining Headquarters, and that the Chief Compound was crowded with employed and unemployed mine workers. This problem had existed for a while, and those responsible in the Chief Compound had been unable to come up with a suitable solution for how to help the mine workers. Of course, the Chiefs always had enough food to feed their dependents while at the same time supporting the needy. The problem in Leleeh's Compound at that time was that they were not organized enough to render help to a large group of people, although they had the means.

The immediate solution Boi Hawa had for this problem was to get her two cousins, Tenneh Mbele and Hannah Tucker, to work with her in every domain in the Chief Compound. Tenneh Mbele was Leleeh's niece who had grown up in Leleeh's Compound since she was a baby. She knew everything about Leleeh's property and wealth, both in Kpangbama and in Gbonjeima. Hannah Tucker, was also Leleeh's niece. She had grown up in Leleeh's Compound, and had never lived anywhere else in the Chiefdom. So, she was also well informed about Leleeh's wealth and property.

These two "Leleeh's children" teamed up with Boi Hawa to form the group of the "Three Sisters" in Leleeh's Compound. The Three Sisters, and Mi Mojama invited the Chiefdom Police Sergeant in the Compound to go with them to Gbonjeima, where most of the food consumed in Chief's Compound was stored. The storage here did not separate the rice and the farm produce used for current consumption, and that for seeding for the next growing season. Luckily, the Three Sisters, with the help of the Police Sergeant, were able to confirm that the Chief had enough food to feed his dependents, give donations and keep the rest for seeding in farming season.

Having the full information on the food in storage in Gbonjeima, and that in storage in both Mi Mojama's and Mi Sahn's kitchens in the Compound, the Three Sisters had double assurance that it was possible for them to continue to feed both the employed and the unemployed mineworkers that came regularly to Leleeh's Compound for food.

Since the titanium mining company and the bauxite mining company started to feed their employees two meals a day, the number of those regularly coming to Leleeh's Compound for food was reduced during the week when they had to go to work. But on weekends, more workers came to the Chief Compound for food.

Camps were built and villages expanded in areas where a large number of workers were needed throughout the week. This made many workers leave the Headquarters for the camps, except those who actually worked with the Europeans and the Americans in their residences up the Hill. Some of the young employees in those days—Michael Johnson, Daniel Musa, Manfred Momoh and a few others—were provided housing facilities in Leleeh's Compound as they were considered security men and essential services workers.

The Three Sisters did relieve Mi Mojama and Mi Sahn of most of their responsibilities of running Leleeh's Compound. They immediately took charge of the cooking and serving of food to all the Compound dwellers, and to those who came for food in the Compound. They assumed the welcoming and serving of friendly, and government visitors. Those visitors who had to stay for a period of time due to the nature of their visit, and qualified for government guest housing assisted to occupy the appropriate guesthouse. Otherwise, there was always a place in the Compound to provide lodging for visitors.

The government agents that came to Kpangbama, in those days, came mainly to assist the mining companies, since it was not easy for them to contact the Ministry of Mines in Freetown for urgent matters. There were times when the Minister of Mines, the Prime Minister, and even the Governor General came to the titanium and bauxite mining area Chiefdoms of Imperri and Gbangbatok to express their support to the miners, and to affirm that mining was absolutely essential for the economic development of the country.

The Three Sisters were well organized. They were a group of willing and hardworking young women. They helped change the way things were done in Leleeh's Compound. In a heavy rainy season, there was water in every container in the Compound. But in the dry season, one could hardly get clean water to drink, or do anything with. The Three Sisters assumed the responsibility to collect water from the stream and fill every water container in the Compound for drinking, cooking, and washing every morning. They equally decided to do general cleaning of the Compound when required, and to sprinkle some water in heavy dust areas in the Compound regularly.

The Three Sisters were not responsible for bring firewood into the Compound for cooking. The messengers of the Compound and the Chiefdom Policemen were responsible for bringing firewood to the Compound for cooking and they were given some reward for it.

Food Gifts

Leleeh was a kind Paramount Chief. He gave generous donations to some people in his Chiefdom who needed it, in particular, seedlings for farming. The workers on his farm regularly produced healthy seeds. He was always willing to share these seeds with some of the farmers who wanted to try his seeds. His assumption was that the higher the quality the seeds the farmers showed, the greater their harvest would likely be. This assumption appeared to be true. Those who regularly got their seeds from the Chief Compound continued to have good harvest in the Chiefdom.

Apart from the economic crops of coffee, cacao, and kola nut that were sold to the merchants along the coast, rice and other farm produce were required mainly for home consumption. There was no market for them. Farmers produced only enough for the consumption of their family and friends. But all of the sudden, when the titanium and the bauxite companies came to the area with a large number of employees, and those looking for mining work, the farmers became quite aware that it was indispensable for them to learn to produce more food, both to consume and to sell, when required.

Leleeh frequently received gifts from the fishermen, hunters, and trappers in the Chiefdom; also of importance, were goats, sheep, and chicken that came to the Compound as a gift from friends.

The Three Sisters were not familiar with how to handle three baskets of raw ocean fish arriving as a gift to the Compound. They had to have both Mi Mojama and Mi Sahn take over. They asked Boi Hawa and her colleagues to sort the baskets of fish into groups of the same kind, and immediately share about half of the fish with relatives and friends. The remaining half was to be preserved and processed for consumption in the Compound. Some of the fish was to be dried, some salted, and the remaining fried and made ready for cooking.

The Three Sisters were very helpful and efficient in running the show in Leleeh's Compound as regards to taking care of others, cooking, serving, and cleaning. But they were lacking in the understanding of the way a Paramount Chief institution operated.

Not quite a week after Leleeh got baskets of fish from the fishermen, a hunter came with a whole deer, as a gift to the Chief. The hunter was asked to butcher the deer. He did it very well. That was a kind of job the Three Sisters were not capable of doing; neither Mi Mojama and Mi Sahn. But they knew very well those who shared in the gifts that came to the Chief Compound—teachers, pastors, Islamic leaders, the elderly, friends, and relatives. These people were not ignored.

Following the fishermen and the deer hunter, Leleeh's Compound was looking forward to receiving some meat from one of the other trappers. Whatever the trappers were likely to bring as a gift to the Chief would be treated in the same way as the other gifts. Leleeh never kept all the gifts to himself; he shared them. The generous gifts that came to Leleeh's Compound were also generously shared with others. The Three Sisters internalized this behaviour.

There were only two types of grades of hunting nets kept in the Compound. The higher grades were intended for hunting bush hogs and deer, while the lower grades were for the smaller creatures. Since the mining companies came to the area, group hunting for men had been almost deserted. The industrious men were kept busy with mining, as well as farm work. But women continued to express interest in group fishing.

The fishing nets in Leleeh's Compound were always kept in good condition. The small size nets were suitable to be used by only one person, while the larger nets by two or three people. The Three Sisters and their relatives in the Compound enjoyed fishing in the streams around Kpangbama. In the dry season, they regularly organized fishing trips to Foinda and Madina where the streams were large, deeper, and tended to have lots of fish breeding there. It was not unusual for them to come home with a basket full of fish each time they went to either Foinda or Madina.

A fishing trip to Gbonjeima usually brought a good quantity of fish to Leleeh's Compound. During the rainy season when the rivers would flood, some types of fish migrated to the flooded ponds where there would be minimum current to lay and hatch their eggs. By the time the season was over, only a small quantity of the fish in the ponds would be able to swim back into the main river. The rest would be harvested by the Chiefdom people.

Leleeh had always been open to the harvesting of the entrapped fish. This was always done by the Three Sisters and the Compound dwellers. They came with their fishing nets and their helpers. They were able to take the quantity of fish they wanted within a period of three hours.

After the Three Sisters had taken what was supposed to go to the Chief compound, the rest of the fish in the ponds was for the entire Chiefdom. The Chiefdom Policemen were always invited to supervise the fishing in those ponds, so that one family did not take more than their share. As usual, the ration that came to Leleeh's Compound was also shared among friends. The school teachers, pastors, and Islamic leaders all got their share from the quantity that came to the Chief Compound.

The Three Sisters became ever enthusiastic about their services in Leleeh's Compound. Their performance in all the areas of running the activities in the

Compound was highly recognized and credited by their father Leleeh, as well as Mi Mojama and Mi Sahn. The services, obedience, honesty and trustworthiness of both Tenneh Mbeleh and Hannah Tucker were hardly noticed by their relatives in the compound. But when Boi Hawa combined their good behaviour with hers, the Three Sisters completely changed Leleeh's Compound.

The young school leavers from distant districts coming to Kpangbama, looking for mining work had continued to increase. They were regularly coming for food in the Chief Compound. Since the companies organized the two meals a day for their employees, many of them were not showing up for meals anymore. However, the Three Sisters had planned to bring more food from Gbonjeima to increase the stock in the Compound since Christmas was coming. There was a regular work stoppage for about a week during Christmas and New Year's. Most likely there would be more mine workers coming to the Compound for food. The B.T.P. workers had a Departmental Christmas Party every year.

The engineering department had recently come and taken away all the hunting nets in the Compound. They had decided on having bush meat for their Christmas Party. After two days of hunting, they had some deer and bush hog. They returned the hunting net, and gave a whole deer to Leleeh. Just as expected, during the Christmas period, the number of those that came for food in the Compound increased. Fortunately, the Compound had a gift of a whole deer from the engineering department of the company, so there was no likelihood of a meat shortage while the demand for food increased. Leleeh's Compound was always ready to provide additional food for the workers when the company was on a shut down.

Christmas at the Compound

Christmastime was always a time of lively celebration in Leleeh's Compound. Since not all the members of the Chiefdom dancing group resided in Kpangbama, except their leader, it was his responsibility to bring his members together for all kinds of festivities, and report to the Chief that his group was ready to perform.

The Chiefdom dancing group was always required to be ready to perform during the Christmas period, the Ramadan prayer period, and when Leleeh was making a trip out of the Chiefdom. For the Christmas celebration in Kpangbama, their performances always started and ended in Leleeh's compound.

When the drumming and the singing began, who did you see dancing first? The

Three Sisters; Boi Hawa, Tenneh Mbeleh, and Hannah Tucker always opened the dancing in Leleeh's Compound. The Three Sisters brought good service, joy and happiness, and merriment to the Chief Compound.

On the occasions of festivity, such as Ramadan and Christmas, the Chiefdom dancing group did not merely entertain people but they also solicited funds for the group. But when they accompanied Leleeh during Paramount Chief meetings or Agricultural shows in Bo Town, they performed only to entertain the Chief and his entourage.

Ancestral Worship was the predominant religion in Sherbro-Mende land, but Islam and the Christian religion continued to grow. Residents in Leleeh's Compound responded highly favourably to Ramadan. During the Muslim month of fasting, some of them fasted only to please the public, but there were others with fervent Islamic belief among them; Mi Mojama and Mi Sahn usually fasted for the entire month. Of the Three Sisters, Boi Hawa was brought up by two powerful and successful Muslim women, Mi Maseray and Mama Yarkai in Bo Town. She had retained the kindness, the tenderness of heart, the personal interest of helping others, and sharing her resources with others from what she learnt from her early upbringing.

The Three Sisters were quite aware that the Ramadan period was a very busy period of the year for them, in terms of cooking and serving food. In addition to the regular food Leleeh's Compound served to the mineworkers, during the period of Ramadan, two communal meals are served twice a day for the Muslims. The first one early every morning at the start of the fasting day, and the second one in the evening, at the end of the fasting day. All these meals needed to be very nutritious and freshly cooked. The Three Sisters were quite informed about that, and were aware that the Islamic Communal Food was to be prepared in the Chief Compound, but served outside the compound in an Islamic Holy Area.

The Three Sisters got up exceptionally early every morning, assisted by other Muslim women to prepare the morning meals. They started equally early toward the evening for the evening meals. This process continued for a month, up to what was known as "Eid al-Fitr", the end of Muslim Month of Fasting.

This day always started with public prayer in the field, followed by communal meals, and the sharing of gifts. The Three Sisters that served the Muslims through Ramadan were rewarded by members of the Mosque of Kpangbama. Then the merriment started with a march past of some of the young Muslims that came directly to greet Leleeh in his Compound, with a hidden motive to solicit funds. The Chief gave them an undisclosed amount of money. They then left the Compound, continuing with the visits to other Muslim Homes.

All of a sudden, the Chiefdom Group started playing a celebration of Ramadan in Leleeh's Compound. The Three Sisters opened the dancing floor, and they were immediately followed by other residents in the in the Compound. In the show of celebrating Ramadan, just as it was for the celebration of Christmas, the Chiefdom Drumming and Singing Group always solicited funds from the participants. The funds the group received were used to replace or repair old equipment.

Chapter 5: Bio Hawa at the Lodge

The Needs of the People

In all his glory as Paramount Chief of Imperri Chiefdom, Leleeh separated his family affairs from the Chiefdom affairs. He strictly obeyed the Provincial Secretary and the District Commissioners who had direct control over the Chiefdom activities. The heads of the Secret Societies—Poro, Bondo, Njayeh and Humoi—consulted with him about whatever they wanted to do in the Chiefdom. His opinion about these Secret Societies was that, as long as their behaviour did not interfere with the peace in the Chiefdom, he would allow them to operate.

Leleeh was judicious, kind, generous, and friendly. He had good humour, and was gentle at heart. His nickname "Leleeh" meant tenderness of heart in Sherbro-Mende. He was able and willing to feed the mineworkers until the Company decided to provide two meals for all the workers who were able to show up in the camps for food. Leleeh had lots of people who depended on him for their sustenance both in the Compound at Kpangbama and in Gbonjeima.

In his capacity as a Chief, he was able to attend to the needs of these people. Some of these people had remarkable improvement in their life by working hard on the farm, and by harvesting and processing Leleeh's cash crop from which they benefited when then it was sold. Among Leleeh's entourage were two outstanding faithfuls—Mi Mojama and Mi Sahn. Whatever idea Leleeh divined, these two powerful women were capable of executing it.

One was to have Mi Mojama take Boi Hawa to Bo Town, and bring her back to Kpangbama only when she was old enough to be initiated into the Secret Bondo Society. While she was awaiting initiation, and after her graduation from the initiation, she helped for a while to improve the running of her father's Compound.

Dr. Margai wanted her to be his wife. The match-making between Dr. Margai and Boi Hawa was done by Mi Sahn. Dr. Margai, then Prime Minister of Sierra Leone, was invited to Kpangbama by both the titanium and the bauxite miners in the area to sign a land agreement. On this matter, the Minister spent long hours in negotiation with his brother, Paramount Chief of Banta Gbanbatok, as well as Leleeh of Imperri Chiefdom. When the Prime Minister finally finished with his official business, his discussion with Leleeh for Boi Hawa to come to Freetown with him continued. Leleeh finally agreed to have Dr. Margai take his daughter as his wife.

The Prime Minister and his Staff Members returned to Freetown. No sooner had they arrived in Freetown, than a vehicle was dispatched to come and get Boi Hawa. There was some delay in getting Boi Hawa to leave for Freetown. Mi Mojama and Mi Sahn wanted not merely bags of rice and farm produce, but also livestock to be part of the provisions that Boi Hawa would take with her. Unfortunately, all of the Leleeh's bulls were too big to get into a government Land Rover. Only a goat was acceptable. And a he-goat was what they got for the trip.

Mi Sahn was to accompany Boi Hawa on her journey to Freetown to join Dr. Margai at the Lodge. On the last-minute preparation for the departure from Leleeh's Compound, Boi Hawa did wear her blue velvet dress she wore during her graduation from the Secret Bondo Society, with her gold ring, earrings, necklace, and gold bracelet. Her two sisters Tenneh Mbeleh and Hannah Tucker helped her load her belongings into the vehicle.

Leleeh, a six-footer, gray hair, in his long gown, drawing smoke from his wooden pipe, and keenly observing what his children were doing, asked, "How many country clothes have you got in your luggage?"

"Only one," responded Boi Hawa.

"Tenneh, go into my house and get a bigger cloth and put it into that luggage," ordered Leleeh. He continued, "On the top of that hill in Freetown, where Dr. Margai is resident, there is regular cold wind blowing there all the time, one has got to be prepared for that."

Everyone in the Compound came out to wave Boi Hawa goodbye as she embraced her father, Mi Mojama, and her mother, Mi Kemah, goodbye. As soon as the vehicle moved, Mi Kemah, who had been wiping tears in her eyes, broke out into a loud cry, weeping for the departure of her only daughter, thinking that she would never see her again.

"Are you going to stop that foolish crying?" Leleeh asked Mi Kemah. "I would like you to serve some food here in the Small Court. I am going to have Tenneh Mbele to have Sanda, Abu Baun, Sumar Keigar, Sam Johnson, and Alpha Barry, to come for food."

"Sanda" was the nickname of the Chiefdom Speaker, Beah Hiteh; Abu Baun was the head of the Section Chiefs; Sumar Keigar was the Assisting Chiefdom Speaker; Sam Johnson was the Resident Civil Servant; and Alpha Barry was the senior of the businessmen in town. Leleeh never ate his meals alone. He always had to have the Chiefdom Speaker, and a combination of his Tribal Authorities and local businessmen share his meals so they could discuss Chiefdom matters and social events. Titanium and bauxite mining brought many foreign workers and young school leavers to the Chiefdom. To keep himself well informed about activities in the Chiefdom he established good connection with reliable people in the Chiefdom and in the mining companies.

Mi Kemah stopped the crying, wiped the tears, and quickly responded to Leleeh's orders. Food was served accordingly. Many events made Sherbro-Mende women cry—accidents, death of a loved one, departure of a loved one to a strange land, or an unexpected surprise. The loud crying of those involved was usually an expression of a mixture of grief and prayers. The prayers were always an appeal to the Ancestors to intervene with the appropriate solution to remove the grief and the sorrow.

Mi Kemah was always suspicious that Dr. Margai was going to take her daughter to a strange, faraway land and that she would be unable to come home. She never stopped appealing to the Ancestors to guide and protect her daughter.

Leleeh himself became uneasy at the departure of Boi Hawa to Freetown. It certainly created a great vacancy in his Compound. But he had to accept the fact that a chief's daughter had to be somebody's wife. She couldn't stay in her father's Compound indefinitely.

Although Leleeh fully agreed to the union of Dr. Margai and his daughter, and was able to bless it, and further made an appeal to the Ancestors to bless and accept the union, he was, however, uneasy about the compatibility of the couple. Dr. Margai, son of a Paramount Chief of Banta Gbangbatok Chiefdom, was once married, when he was in Medical School in the United Kingdom. But his wife and two daughters had never come with him when he returned to Sierra Leone. Since then, he had been Senior

Medical Officer of the country, founder of a political party The Sierra Leone People's Party (SLPP), of which he was the Chaiman, and then Prime Minister of the country. Dr. Margai was definitely an academic, and a great achiever.

Boi Hawa was, equally, daughter of the Paramount Chief of Imperri Chiefdom (Leleeh). She had barely Middle School education, but was exposed to strong traditional upbringing by Mi Maseray and Mama Yarkai in Bo Town. When she returned to Kpangbama, she was initiated into the Sacred Bundo Society. This was the time of the influx of the titanium and bauxite miners in the Chiefdom. She immediately took charge of running her father's Compound, and helped provide sustenance for the stranded mineworkers. She was friendly, polite, sometimes timid in the company of others, but quick to build new relationships.

Despite the many discrepancies that appeared in Leleeh's thoughts that might be of detriment to the union between Dr. Margai and Boi Hawa, there was one fundamental similarity that held them together; the both of them were children of Paramount Chiefs of neighbouring Chiefdoms that had maintained cordial relationship since time immemorial.

The departure of Boi Hawa to Freetown was finalized between Leleeh and Dr. Margai when he returned home after his business meetings with the mining companies. Dr. Margai sent a vehicle to collect Boi Hawa as soon as he got to Freetown. Leleeh then had Boi Hawa, accompanied by Mi Sahn, immediately leave for Freetown. The sudden departure of Boi Hawa and Mi Sahn created some vacancy in the Compound in the areas that were wholly dependent on her and the team of the Three Sisters (Boi Hawa, Tenneh Mbeleh, and Hannah Tucker)—collecting water from the stream to the Compound for drinking, cooking and washing; collecting firewood; general cleaning of the Compound; and, cooking. These responsibilities squarely remained in the hands of Tenneh Mbeleh and Hannah Tucker. They were able to serve Leleeh's Compound to his satisfaction.

A week after Boi Hawa left for Freetown, Leleeh received a message from Dr. Margai that Mi Sahn, who had accompanied Boi Hawa to Freetown, was going to stay a little longer at the Lodge to help Boi Hawa. She had to learn to deal with house maids, and other servants who had been at the Lodge for a long time and were familiar with the proceedings, but had become directly answerable to her. Having Mi Sahn on her side, they were able to establish a convenient way for the new House Wife of the Prime Minister to deal with the servants of the house. The individual responsibilities of the house maids, and the servants were defined and clarified, so that Boi Hawa was able to monitor their performances. This was only in relation to family members of the Prime Minister.

The house maids and servants at the Lodge were government employees. They were quite obedient and respectful to the Prime Minister's family members, consequently, the Prime Minister's wife had no problems in her dealings with them. Each one of them had his or her job description and specifications to which they attended during their working hours with the utmost care. And each of them did seek Boi Hawa's approval in their daily activities at the Lodge.

Boi Hawa did not have to worry about managing security staff of the Lodge. The Lodge was fully protected by the Sierra Leone Military. And all incoming and outgoing information to and from the Prime Minister's Residence was under the control of Civil Servants.

The situation here was much easier and convenient compared to what she was used to in her father's Compound. Being the eldest daughter in the family, she had to plan, organize, and also take part in daily vital duties, including cleaning, cooking, and attending to important visitors to the Chief Compound.

Boi Hawa Kpanabom was a very intelligent woman. Elevated from a Sherbro-Mende Native Paramount Chief Compound to the Prime Minister's Residence, the Lodge, as the Prime Minister's wife, she quickly adapted to the new lifestyle and the environment. In a very short time, she was able to easily and brilliantly play the role of the Prime Minister's wife. The family members and domestic servants at the Lodge that reported to her respectfully obeyed her commands.

She was a powerful woman in terms of the services she rendered to others, friendly, and observant. She used her kindness as an instrument to gain others' trust so they were willing to do things for her. Through her impressive performance at the Lodge, Dr. Margai realized that it was not necessary to keep Mi Sahn as her helper. Consequently, another messenger was sent to Leleeh in Kpangbama to inform him Mi Sahn was due to return home during Christmastime.

One week before Christmas each year, Dr. Margai would go to Gbangbatok to spend the Christmas with his brother, Paramount Chief Margai and members of their extended family. This year was no exception. He came with his entire family, including a few security men and dependable servants. That same day, Mi Sahn was accompanied to Kpangbama.

On her arrival at the Compound in Kpangbama, Mi Sahn went straight to the Small Court Building, where Leleeh was lying in his hammock smoking his wooden.

"Welcome home, after a long stay in Freetown!" Leleeh received Mi Sahn. "What's in this luggage?"

Mi Sahn was slow to respond to Leleeh's questions. She appeared tired following a long trip from Freetown. Eventually, she took some strength to respond to Leleeh's queries.

"I have here three different bottles of drinks for you sent by Dr. Margai. I guess this first bottle is a whiskey, the second one is surely a gin, and then a rum. In addition, he gave me 50 Pounds cash and Boi Hawa also gave me 10 Pounds cash. I have used this money to buy a print and a head tie for Mi Mojama, Mi Kemah, and also for myself."

"What did you buy for me?" Leleeh further enquired. But Mi Sahn had no response for him.

After Mi Sahn had taken her leave from Leleeh, he sent Tenneh Mbeleh to call her to come back to the Small Court. He had planned to reciprocate the Christmas gifts he had received from Dr. Margai.

"Is it possible for us to give two goats to both Paramount Chief Margai and Dr. Margai for their Christmas?" Leleeh asked Mi Sahn on her arrival.

"Yes. We can," responded Mi Sahn. "We have many goats being raised at Gbonjeima."

"Please arrange to have two goats sent to both P.C. Margai and Dr. Margai at Gbangbatok for their Christmas." Mi Sahn executed this order immediately.

In Gbangbatok, Banta Chiefdom, people talk about Christmas Week and New Year Week. The residents enjoyed the festivities at the end of every year. Dr. Margai, the Prime Minister of Sierra Leone, came every year to join his brother, the P.C. of the Chiefdom to celebrate. In anticipation of the arrival of the Prime Minister, sections of the Chiefdom organized a general hunting for a fat deer and a fat boar to be presented to the Chief for his brother, for the year-end festivities. This same generosity of the residents of the Chiefdom was equally responded to by residents from down river, along the Atlantic Coast, who equally provided fresh fish, fried fish and dried fish for each end of year occasion.

On her first visit to Gbangbatok with her husband for Christmas and the New Year weeks, Boi Hawa did highly appreciate the generosity of the Chiefdom People. Raised in the neighbouring Chief Compound of Imperri Chiefdom, she had no problem mingling with the wives Chief Margai. They cooked together, and served the food to family members, and the many visitors that showed up for the occasions together.

During the drumming and the singing in P.C. Margai's Compound, she did join in with the Chief's wives in dancing and she made some contributions to the musicians, which they highly appreciated, and they sang her name aloud, making mention of her father "Leleeh".

In every event of these celebrations, Chief Margai made available a good supply of Nduvui Wine, from Pabarma, local wine tapped from Nduvui Palm; and Palm Wine, tapped from Oil Palm Tree. The entire population enjoyed these drinks. But the Prime Minister's wife did not drink a drop.

Dr. Margai and his brother enjoyed watching people dancing but never showed up on a dancing floor. The both of them showed great interest in the Kongoli and Gondeh performances. Kongoli, broad faced, oversized nose, mouth, lips and dental structure, was considered the male crown; while the female crown, Gondeh, despite the fact that she carried the same head as the normal Sacred Bondo Devil, she appeared covered by a bizarre costume that her audience could see her almost half naked. She performed and behaved completely opposite to the way the Sacred Bondo Devil did, and in contradiction to what a well-behaved Sherbro-Mende woman could do. Kongoli, on the other hand, danced and had his own songs to sing and cracked jokes for his audience.

Both Gondeh and Kongoli, in all their appearances, always tried to present the life of a man in their own ways. When Kongoli and Gondeh had the opportunity to perform, they usually did the extraordinary that others did not do on the stage. Just as much as they improvised in their costumes they brought to the show, they also spontaneously entertained and amused their audience to laughter. Dr. Margai and his brother spent long hours being entertained by Kongoli and Gondeh.

The Quest for Independence

Back in Freetown, after the Christmas holidays, was the general election in Sierre Leone. Dr. Margai was aware that he had a powerful woman who had the capacity to help him and the entire Sierra Leone People's Party in the election. The S.L.P.P. at this time had two other opposing political parties all based in Freetown. As a result, the appropriate battlegrounds for the election were in the Provinces of Sierra Leone and not the City of Freetown.

The Prime Minister and his wife took the election campaign straight into the District Headquarters, Chiefdom Headquarters and all the large towns in each Chiefdom. It was in Sumbuya, one of the mining towns in the Bo District, that the Prime Minister's wife was interrupted by an intruder while campaigning.

"What is Leleeh's daughter doing here?" asked the intruder. He had definitely been sent by one of the opposing party candidates. In some of the Chiefdom headquarters, it was not unusual for someone to ask Boi Hawa, "Are you not Leleeh's daughter?"

"Yes, I am," she would usually respond. "But I am now the Prime Minister's wife."

It was a short election campaign designed to test the support of the country for the Prime Minister, and his party. S.L.P.P. had a landslide victory. The Prime Minister's wife played a remarkable role in the election campaign.

When the Sierra Leone Parliament resumed after the election, a Constitutional Council was voted to draw up the Constitution for the Independence of Sierra Leone in the Commonwealth. The Council was made up of Paramount Chiefs, parliamentarians, colonial officials, and national legal experts. After drawing up the Constitution having it accepted by parliament, and making it public to the nation, the Sierra Leone Government requested constitution talks from the British Government. This request was quickly granted and a date set for the talks.

In their final preparation for their trip to London for the independence negotiations, Parliament selected a certain number of persons from each political party to constitute a group called the "United Front" to represent the Sierra Leone Government in London, England. Before the "United Front" left Freetown for London, the Prime Minister had to be there for preliminary meetings with the British parliamentarians.

In all his itinerary in the Nation as regards political campaigning—opening of school, mines, bridges, general party meetings or agricultural shows—the Prime Minister went with his wife. But during his oversea engagements, he regularly travelled with his personal bodyguards and his confidential secretary. On arrival in a foreign country, the host countries took over the security of their guest during their stay up to the time of their departure. Any time the Prime Minister had to leave for a trip abroad, his wife assumed the complete responsibility of the family at the Lodge as well as those in Gbanbgatok.

The Constitutional Talks in London were unusually long. It took much more time than expected. At home, people were becoming skeptical about the possible outcome of this negotiation. During this uncertain period, the Prime Minister's wife had lots problems to respond to at the Lodge, Gbangbatok, and Kpangbama, the paternal home of the Prime Minister's wife. But she was a strong and a clever woman.

The Sierra Leone Constitutional Negotiation for Independence almost failed. The United Front got into a dispute that was unsolvable. The members of the All People's Congress Party broke off from the United Front and returned home prematurely, refusing to give their support to Sierra Leone's Independence. However, the British Parliament accepted the Sierra Leone Constitution with the willingness to grant independence at any acceptable future date. The Prime Minister and the rest of his delegation returned home from London triumphantly. The entire nation gave them a hearty welcome. There was jubilation in the Nation.

New Ways Forward

The Colonial Officials were in support of Dr. Margai becoming the Head of State in Sierra Leone. They gave their full assistance in all sectors of the economy—in colleges, private and public schools—to make the population aware of what the independence of a nation meant, that the colonial masters would be gone, and that the Nation had to assume all their responsibilities on their own.

The Sierra Leone Parliament was not in haste to set the date for Independence. They were more anxious for the population to fully understand the changes that were coming in the Nation.

During this interlude, Leleeh became sick and was brought to Freetown for treatment. Dr. Margai admitted him at the Lodge for observation, but his condition became serious and he was taken to the Government Hospital where he did pass away. This situation brought a sudden obstacle at the Lodge.

The Prime Minister had just came home after an unusually long stay in London, and his wife had to go to Mbeleh Town to bury her father. She was required to go through all the traditional rituals during her father's burial ceremony since she was designated to be her father's successor as Paramount Chief of the Imperri Chiefdom. To ease the burden on the family, Dr. Margai took a week off his busy schedule and went to Leleeh's burial at Mbeleh Town. He made a short tribute to the life of the late Paramount Chief Kpanabom to the immediate family members, spent two days at the Rutile Mines at Kpangbama, and then, to Gbangbatok his home, where he spent the rest of his time off, and then returned to work in Freetown.

The whole ritual of Leleeh's funeral was held in Mbeleh Town, where he was buried by the Poro Society, the original base of the Sacred Societies in the Chiefdom, as regards, Poro, Njayeh and Humoi. His house was used as the funeral home where the immediate family members, led by Mi Naneh, Mi Mojama, Mi Sahn and others to mourn for Leleeh. Boi Hawa Kpanabom, the Prime Minister's wife was not allowed to join this group, since she had two young children at this time, and had other demanding family responsibilities. However, since she was the would-be successor of her father, she had to be around this group to greet and receive the sympathizers.

For the first three days after the burial, the immediate family members continued to cry in the evenings, midnights, and in the mornings. The crying at Leleeh's funeral by his family and friends was not merely a grieving process, but also a prayer process. The crying individuals would appeal to the Ancestors to open the way for Leleeh, and receive him in their fold. That crying continued up to the three days' ceremony. After that, the Prime Minister's wife returned to Freetown. She came back for the seven days' ceremony.

The Tribal Authorities of the Chiefdom wanted Boi Hawa to stay in the Chiefdom up to the forty days' ceremony, so that she could start her campaign for the Chieftaincy. But her husband, the Prime Minster was not willing for her to do that. What was feasible at the time was for her to come to the Chiefdom for a day or two every two or three weeks until the ceremony.

Following the forty days' ceremony, the Regent Chief was quickly selected by the Central Government. Leleeh's Chiefdom Speaker was selected as Regent Chief. During the Regency, some activities returned to the old Chief Compound. Mi Mojama and Mi Sahn returned to their houses. The family court sessions were held in the small court during the Regency, just as they were during Leleeh's time. The Regent Chief assigned security men to guard all the valuable property in the Compound.

During Christmas that year, the Prime Minister, as usual, was at Gbangbatok with the rest of his family to spend the Christmas. The day after Christmas, Boi Hawa went to Kpangbama with her Christmas present for the relatives there. The town was full of mine workers who had known her during the time they were looking for work in the mines, especially the school leavers in those days. Some of these workers surely remembered her kindness in providing them sustenance from the Chief Compound until they were employed.

During this short visit, Boi Hawa was in a campaigning mood for the Chieftaincy.

She visited the Regent Chief, and had invited some Tribal Authorities to come for their Christmas presents. She was joined by her two sisters Tenneh Mbeleh and Hannah Tucker. The "Three Sisters" of fame in old Leleeh's Compound attended the mine workers' organized Christmas Dance. They were well received. Some workers shouted the name "Boi Hawa Kpanabom Paramount Chief of Imperri Chiefdom". Her favourite Salia Record was played, she and her two sisters danced, and the rest of the crowd joined in with them. She gave the mine workers their Christmas gift.

This was a very busy time in the history of Sierra Leone when the Colonial Administrators were recruiting the nationals to be able to run their country themselves after the Independence of their country. When the Prime Minister returned to Freetown from the Christmas Holidays, early in the New Year, the Paramount Chief election for Imperri Chiefdom, Bonthe District was called. All the aspiring candidates registered, but they were all disqualified, including the star candidate, Boi Hawa Kpanabom, the Prime Minister's wife, who was considered the successor of her father. The only candidates that were allowed to take part in this election were those from the Kpangbaia Section. This decision came directly from the Attorney General to the Provincial Secretary who was to conduct the election. The Attorney General's decision was based on formal accepted practice in the Chiefdom that the Chieftaincy in the Imperri Chiefdom rotate from Mbeleh Section, to Kpangbaia Section, Gendema Section, Victoria, Mo-King, and Mo-Maligue. This was definitely the time for Kpangbaia.

The candidates from the Kpangbaia Section made their appeal to the Tribal Authorities in the Chiefdom, and eventually elected the Paramount Chief for the Chiefdom. But some of the elders in the Kpangbaia Section disagreed with the election on the basis that the person elected was not the most qualified. His aunts and uncles were better qualified for the position of Paramount Chief in the Chiefdom. Consequently, he was overthrown and replaced by his aunt.

Chapter 6: Rotational Chieftaincy in Imperri Chiefdom

History of the Chieftaincy

From where did this rotational chieftaincy in the Imperri Chiefdom originate? Why had it become formally accepted over the years? There is certainly a myriad of answers to these questions, and different knowledgeable people have different opinions about this situation.

First of all, the most popular known rotation of the Imperri Chieftaincy had been that between Kpangbaia Chiefs, the Gendema Chiefs, and the Mbeleh Chiefs. However, other parts of the Chiefdom had been presenting candidates for the Paramount Chief position, who were definitely qualified, but unsuccessful.

The claim of the Kpangbaia Section on the Chieftaincy in Imperri was genuine. The town of Kpangbaia itself is situated at the head of the Kpangbaia Tributary that was linked with many bush roads leading very far into the Hinterland that provided prosperous trading possibilities. During the influx of settlers along the Sherbro River, Kpangbaia became one of the favourite areas settled by merchants and tradesmen. The fertile land for farming, the commodities and the farm produce they got from this area made the settlers wealthy. They produced for the export market and sold their food to the neighbouring islands and in Freetown.

It was easy for the American missionaries, who already had a church in Shenge along the Sherbro River, to establish in Kpangbaia. They built a church, a school, a hospital and a mission house. From there, the Mission continued to expand further into the Hinterland.

The Chiefs of Mbeleh took advantage of this development in their Chiefdom and started to send their children to Kpangbaia to learn. Some families even relocated to the area to work for the merchants and some for the Mission. The offspring of families from Mbeleh, who had the right to the Imperri Chieftaincy, had always defended their right and had been successful in being elected as Paramount Chiefs of the Imperri Chiefdom, under the connotation of Kpangbaia Chiefs, mainly due to their education and acquired culture.

The Imperri Chiefdom Chieftaincy claim by the offspring of those Chiefs who relocated to Gendema from Mbeleh is similar to those who relocated to Kpangbaia. Gendema, located near the Atlantic Coast was settled by many farmers, merchants and tradesmen. This area did produce timber, vegetable oil and food for the export market. It attracted workers from the Hinterland that worked on the farms, harvested and collected palm fruits, and worked as sawyers. Most families in Gendema sent their children to school in Bonthe Town, and many were able to send their children to schools in Freetown.

Those families that had their children go into the ships as sailors, or to England to study, became very wealthy through the support of their children. And since this section of the Chiefdom had easy access to markets in the Islands and in Freetown, as well as the export market for their vegetable oil, timber and the animal skins that they produced, most families were well off, compared to the rest of the Chiefdom. Those Mbeleh offspring in Gendema that had right for the Imperri Chieftaincy had been able to be elected as Paramount Chiefs of Imperri Chiefdom, under the connotation of Gendema Chiefs. Their wealth, acquired culture, and education had influenced their election.

Many people argue that the origin of the rotation of the Imperri Chieftaincy had come from the relocation of Chief families to economically and commercially developed areas in the Chiefdom, who, through intermarriage, acquired culture, education and wealth were able to lay claims on their inherent right in the Chiefdom. And these claims were accepted and approved by the Colonial Government. In this case, one would take for granted that the right of these families was tied to their person, and that they had the authority to defend this right anywhere in the Chiefdom, as long as the Colonial Government approved of them.

There was, however, some argument against the economic migrants or the relocated Chief offspring in Kpangbaia and in Gendema, and also those Imperri Chieftaincy contestants who never wanted to identify themselves with Mbeleh Town or Mbeleh Section. These people considered their right to the Imperri Chiefdom

Chieftaincy was tied to their person, so that they could be Kpangbaia Chiefs, or Gendema Chiefs ruling the Imperri Chiefdom. They ignored the fact that the inherent right or birthright of a Chief was tied to a piece of land in a given location, that was Mbeleh Town or Mbeleh Section, which could not be transferred to another location through marriage, education, wealth or acquired culture. However, their position had received the support and approval of the Colonial Administration. This situation made Imperri Chiefdom, although a unitary Chiefdom, appear to be a kind of amalgamated Chiefdom.

Those who had knowledge about this chieftaincy rotation in the Imperri Chiefdom had always argued that the Colonial Administration had had some acceptance and rejection of the Imperri Chiefdom, in particular, having Mbeleh Town or Mbeleh Section as the only area for sourcing the Paramount Chief for the entire Chiefdom.

Imperri Chiefdom was highly favoured by the settlers along the Sherbro River, mainly because it presented great economic prospect to the newcomers. It had navigable rivers going deep into the Hinterland that were easily settled by the merchants and traders; it had timber land for sawyers, fertile farmland and commodities for the export market. These settlers were followed by missionaries who built churches and schools, and went further, preaching the Gospel to the natives in the Hinterland.

The Chiefdom became very active and resourceful in producing food in the country and commodities for the export market. In order to promote more development in the Chiefdom, the Colonial Government built the first Commissioner's Residence and a Frontier Police Force Barracks in the Chiefdom, outside the domain of the Colony, that became known as the "Tribal District of Imperri". The Commissioner's Quarters and the Frontier Police Barracks were both built in Kpangbama, which eventually became the new Chiefdom Headquarters, abandoning Mbeleh Town and Mbeleh Section.

Despite the great economic opportunities that Imperri Chiefdom presented to the Colonial Government, and the wealth the merchants were making from the resources of this Chiefdom, the Colonial Government continued to reject the natives of Mbeleh Town or Mbeleh Section from having access to their Chieftaincy. Their preference was for the educated, the wealthy, and those with adopted culture; the offspring of those Chiefs that had relocated to economically suitable areas in the Chiefdom, like Kpangbaia, Gendema, Momaligue, Victoria, Mo-King, and Jangalor. The Colonial

Administrators considered that the Chiefs from Mbeleh Section were highly committed Sacred Societies such as Poro, Nyayeh, and Humoi; consequently, they rejected progress, remained superstitious, uncivilized, ignorant, and fetishistic. They had to be kept as far away from the Chieftaincy as possible. When the Chieftaincy rotated, it might fall to them, probably, once every one hundred years.

There was some serious contention between the Colonial Administration and some of the Sections of the Chiefdom, Imperri included, that the rotation of the Chieftaincy in a Unitary Chiefdom was not appropriate because it weakened the Sacred Societies that had always protected and defended the Chiefdom from invasion of enemies. But the Colonial Administration rejected this argument by confirming that the rotation of the Chieftaincy was more suitable for the Chiefdom. Consequently, the rotation of the Paramount Chieftaincy became accepted by all, at the detriment of weakening the base of the Sacred Societies.

Unfortunately, during the Hut Tax War, the Mbeleh Poro Society was unable to stop the Warboys. The Warboys were a group of fighters who waged war against missionaries, foreign settlers, merchants, and government agencies during the Hut Tax War. They attacked the Frontier Police Barracks, killing all the policemen, the Resident Commissioner and all his dependents. Then they demolished the church, the school, the mission house, and the hospital at Kpangbaia. The Sacred Poro Society was able to save the lives of the American missionaries who were in charge of the Mission at Kpangbaia. They did compromise with the Poro Society up to the end of the war.

After the war, the Governor had his revenge on the Warboys and their supporters without trial. He killed over one hundred of them and sent some of the chiefs into exile. The Governor then appointed the American missionary, Daniel Flickinger Wilberforce as Paramount Chief of the Imperri Chiefdom. He was considered a compromising person that would help to rebuild the country after the Hut Tax War. He made Victoria his Chiefdom Headquarters, where he built a school and a church. He rebuilt Kpangbaia, and built a girl's boarding school in Bonthe. He appealed to more American missionaries to come to Sierra Leone for mission work. He eventually retired and returned to America.

Paramount Chief Daniel Flickinger Wilberforce

During his time in office as Paramount Chief of Imperri Chiefdom, Daniel Flickinger Wilberforce played the role of rebuilder and reconciliator. Since the damage done to the government property in the Chiefdom was extensive, he never tried to rebuild or repair them. However, he repaired churches and schools that were damaged, and also built new ones. He did build a church and a school in Mbeleh Town, but he never went there. He was in Kpangbama only for Chiefdom Court matters. All other Chiefdom meetings were held in Victoria.

Apart from the time the Chief spent in the Mission House in Freetown, and in Bonthe where he built another mission house, he spent most of his time in Gendema, Jangalor, Mo-King, Momaligue and Kpangbaia. These towns had many new settlers, merchants and tradesmen, some of whom had been seriously affected by the war. The farm produce and the commodities that were produced from these areas were essential for both the export market and for home consumption. Given the growing commercial activities along the Sherbro River, and the protection provided by the Government for businesses that survived the war, the situation got back to normal quickly. Other towns, including Sumbuya, Gambia, Mattru Jong, Babar, and Bo-Njembui did join in the export trade through their heavy production palm produce and timber.

Chief Daniel Flickinger Wilberforce clearly demonstrated that rotational Chieftaincy was acceptable in the Imperri Chiefdom. He spent more time and government money in these areas in the Chiefdom that were economically developed, and where the offspring of Mbeleh Chiefs had claims on the Chieftaincy, forgetting the fact that Chieftaincy was tied to a piece of land that could not be relocated, and that, if one wanted to become a chief, one had to return to his or her roots. However, since the Colonial Administration had in the past granted Chieftaincy to contenders in this situation, he totally tried to enforce it.

Apart from the tendency of electing Chiefs among the educated, the wealthy, and those with adopted cultures, there was no justification for the Chieftaincy in the Imperri Chiefdom to be rotational. The Chiefdom was unitary and not amalgamated. That simply meant that all the claimant for the position of Paramount Chieftaincy had to do was have their roots in Mbeleh Town and Mbeleh Section. There was no justification for Chieftaincy rotation in the Imperri Chiefdom. Any candidate that wanted to contest for the Chieftaincy in this chiefdom would have to start from Mbeleh Town where all claims should start, "the root". The Attorney General would look into this matter seriously.

The Quest for Independence

The avid ambition of Boi Hawa Kpanabom to succeed her father as Paramount Chief of the Imperri Chiefdom while, at the same time, remaining a loving and supporting wife of her husband, the Prime Minister of Sierra Leone failed, due to the rotational nature of the Chieftaincy in the Imperri Chiefdom. All the contestants in this election were disqualified, except those that registered under the Kpangbaia Section.

The Prime Minister's wife returned to the Lodge with mixed feelings, that the Attorney General needed to probe seriously into this matter, and also continued to express willingness to concentrate on supporting her husband's political career rather than to be involved in additional Native Administration affairs. This was the time of Sierra Leone Independence. The Prime Minister needed all the support he could possibly get from his wife to organize and attend parties and entertain friends.

While the Sierra Leone People's Party, the entire Government, and the Prime Minister and his wife were involved in having every village and every town in the country join in the hype of the country's newfound Independence, the Colonial Administrators had, for a period of time, turned their attention to the new national economy. The mining companies, as regards diamond, gold, bauxite, titanium, and iron ore were in full production and exporting; the same was applicable to commodities and farm produce both for home consumption and for the export market.

The coordination between the Colonial Administrators and the national politicians to put people to work, to socially develop the nation and to grow the economy proved to be very successful. During this period of Prime Minister Milton Margai's Government, there was prosperity. The new nation was heading in the direction of developed ones. The institutions inherited from the Colonial Administration were functioning perfectly well. The acceptable performance of Sierra Leone after independence, the role the new nation was playing in the British Commonwealth of Nations, the state of the economy, and the peace that existed there, did not go unnoticed by the Queen of England. Within a short time after becoming the head of state of Sierra Leone, Dr. Margai was invited to London by the Queen of England for Knighthood. He was knighted by the Queen of England for his service to Sierra Leone in the Commonwealth of Nations.

Dr. Milton Margai, the Head of State of Sierra Leone immediately acquired the title "Sir" and became known as Sir Milton Margai for life. One would imagine that the wife would take the title of Madam Margai, but that never happened. Behind every successful man there are always wonderful women, their mothers who bring them up to be achievers, and their wives who made their beds, fed them and led them to achievement in life. This was quite indicative of the performance of Boi Hawa Kpanabom when she became the wife of Dr. Milton Margai.

She came to the Lodge when Sir Milton was the Chairman and the leader of the S.L.P.P., the political party he jointly founded with his friends. At the Lodge, she had to work with family members, domestic servants and civil service personnel, all in the perfect interests of her husband. Dr. Margai then became the Prime Minister after an overwhelming election victory with the support of his wife. This election was followed by constitutional talks in London which granted the Colony of Sierra Leone the status of an Independent State in the Commonwealth of Nations. Dr. Margai, then, successfully achieved his goal of becoming the first Head of State of Sierra Leone.

Where did the wife of Dr. Milton Margai, Boi Hawa Kpanabom acquire the skills of helping to elevate her husband to the position of Head of State and eventually a Knighthood, one of the first Sierra Leoneans ever knighted? The wife of Sir Milton Margai was one of those young girls in Bo Town, who regularly went to collect clean drinking water for Mama Yarkai from the Kobongoi Stream, and also went to get firewood from Kendeyama village for cooking group meals during the fast months of the Ramadan.

In her father's Compound in Kpangbama, as a young woman, initiated into the Sacred Bondo Society, she regularly did all the cleaning, fetched firewood for cooking and drinking water from the stream. During the early days of rutile and bauxite mining in the area, which brought a large number of school leavers without housing and food, she provided food for those who needed it until they were employed by the mining companies. Boi Hawa Kpanabom was kind, friendly, generous and supportive to others.

The Royal Visit

The Royal Visit to the nation brought tremendous honour and respect to Sierra Leone. It served as recognition and confidence of the Queen of England and the Commonwealth of Nations in the Head of State and his people. Sierra Leone as a new nation in the Commonwealth of Nations, and Sir Milton Margai was highly elevated when Sierra Leone was honoured to host the Royal Visit. Of equal importance to Sir

Milton Margai's family was that his daughter, with Boi Hawa Kpanabom, Sally Margai was selected by Parliament to welcome the Royal Visitors to Sierra Leone. The people of the Bonthe District, and in particular those of the Imperri Chiefdom were delighted to hear that the granddaughter of P.C. Kpanabom was to welcome the Queen of England to Sierra Leone.

The Royal Visit further stimulated economic activities in Sierra Leone. New roads were constructed, old roads resurfaced, and old government buildings renovated. New government projects were quickly put into place to renovate some schools, hospitals, playgrounds, and guest houses. The mines, in particular; diamond, gold, rutile and bauxite mines, were provided funding to renovate their guest houses for the visitors and tourists. Paramount Chiefs in all the Chiefdoms put together a gift package for the Royals. They planned individual shows and group shows to entertain the visitors. Dancing groups from various Chiefdoms performed at different places as was required. The visitors were really entertained by the traditional, cultural display and the black magic.

The Royal Visit was not only a stimulant to the national economy, but it assisted in bringing new ideas into the developing nation. Government and foreign grants were increased to schools and colleges to build new classrooms and laboratories. British Council expanded their services in Freetown as well as in the provinces. Public library services were equally increased throughout the nation. Cultural dancing groups were developed, and organized to the level that they went on a very successful world tour.

What else did Sierra Leone require from Sir. Milton Margai? He became ill. And he died.

Widowhood

His rich widow, Boi Hawa Kpanabom, was supposed to settle in Freetown, but did not like the environment. She left for the family home of her late husband, where Sir Milton Margai's brother was the Paramount Chief. This was nearer her home, Kpangbama, her place of birth. While residing in Gbangbatok, she visited home several times and had her childhood bedroom in the "board house" renovated for her to stay, whenever she came home. But neither Gbangbatok nor Kpangbama were the places that she wanted to stay at that time.

She finally decided to reside in Bonthe, where she opened a retail business and went into partnership with one of the successful businessmen in town, and they eventually got married. Their retail business prospered, and they expanded into the commodity export business along the Sherbro River. The piassava export business became their main domain, but they did handle other commodities and farm produce for export.

When Paramount Chief Madam Njabu, the Chief that was elected after Leleeh, passed away, the tribal authorities in the Chiefdom immediately sent a delegation to Boi Hawa Kpanabom that they wanted her as the next Paramount Chief of the Imperri Chiefdom. Meanwhile, a Regent Chief was selected by the Government to run the Chiefdom until they were ready for the election.

The Regent Chief had many problems to solve in the Chiefdom before handing over for Paramount Chief election. The local court system in the Chiefdom had not been functioning for a while because of the lack of a Court Chairman. The documents for the local tax collection were not available. It was believed that the tax collection was three periods behind the normal local tax time. And the treasury clerk was nowhere to be found in the Chiefdom. The Regent Chief had to put things in order in such a situation before asking the Government for Chiefdom election.

There was a need to select a Court Chairman, have him approved by the Tribal Authorities, trained and put to work. The Regent Chief did this job in an extremely urgent manner. The accounting technicians in the mining company assisted the Regent Chief with the local tax collection in the Chiefdom because they had previous records on file about the local taxes collection. These records would not have changed within a short period of time.

Those in the position of authority in the Chiefdom played their roles in helping the Regency get the Chiefdom well organized and ready for the election of a new Paramount Chief. The mining companies in the Chiefdom wanted a substantive Chief in office to deal with instead of a Regent. Those who expected a long Regency in the Chiefdom were disappointed. The highly efficient Regent Chief, selected by the Government, was able to get the Chiefdom ready for election within the shortest possible time.

When the Attorney General called the Paramount Chief election in the Imperri Chiefdom, which was conducted by the Provincial Secretary, Boi Hawa Kpanabom was elected. Officially crowned as Madam Hawa Kpanabom Soukan, she became immediately popularly known as "Mama Hawa". As per tradition, she assumed the position of the head of all the Sacred Societies in the Chiefdom. There was a formal libation in her honour, an appeal to the Ancestors to receive her, lead, guide, and protect her in all her leadership functions.

Mama Hawa got into office at the best of times. The mining companies in the area were expanding production and increasing shipments of their products. The miners closely collaborated with the Chief and helped in rebuilding her Compound to the way her late father had his. Subsequently, the urgency in the expansion of the Rutile Mine was heading toward the venerable Mbeleh Town and Mbeleh Poro Bush, an area where the Colonial Administrators considered sending people who were ignorant, superstitious, uncivilized, rejected progress, and demonstrated fetishes. Mama Hawa, whose roots were from Mbeleh Town, made this stigma disappear. She negotiated with the Rutile Mining Company to have both Mbeleh Town and the Poro Bush removed from the mining activities. The richest known, natural rutile deposit was found in this location.

Mama Hawa was loved and appreciated by her people. She used her personal wealth to give support to the churches, mosques and schools. She took refuge in Bonthe, and eventually in Freetown when the rebels took over the whole country. All People's Congress Party (A.P.C.) had power for nearly thirty years. They had a one-party system with a Republican Constitution, and got rid of all the vital institutions the country inherited from the Colonial Administration, such as the Produce Marketing Board, the Rice Corporation, the Railway, private ownership of the diamond and iron mines.

The Central Committee of the A.P.C. got into a dispute wherein some senior members wanted to get rid of the one political party system and become democratic. Others wanted to retain the one political party system in order to try their chances at becoming president of Sierra Leone. When the democrats, with the aim of a multiparty system continued to advance with the support of foreign powers, the opposing group selected their leader, named Foday Sankor, and asked for an alliance with the neighbouring counties, Liberia and Guinea. Through the support of the Liberian and Guinean soldiers, Foday Sankor was able to take over the whole country for five years. The Rutile Mining Company had to deploy hired foreign soldiers to liberate the mining area of the Imperri Chiefdom from the rebels.

Five years in exile, Mama Hawa came home empty handed, with only the zeal to continue to serve her people. Some people were killed by the rebels, some died during the rebel occupation. Some of those people who had left the rebel-occupied areas never came back. The farmers, in particular who came back to their villages had serious problems in cleaning up after the rebels and starting life anew. The Chiefdom and the mining company gave some helping hands to those who needed them.

Mama Hawa was a clever woman, strong in will, modest, and kind. Being the head of the Sacred Societies in the Chiefdom, she helped demystify the venerability of Mbeleh Town, and Mbeleh Poro Bush, and she was able to facilitate their removal by the Rutile Mining Company. Her husband was the Head of State of Sierra Leone and a Knight in the British Empire, Sir Milton Margai. Her daughter, Sally Margai, welcomed the Queen of England, Elizabeth II, to Sierra Leone during the Royal Visit. The President of Sierra Leone, Madam Boi came to the Imperri Chiefdom for her burial. She had two Margai boys and a daughter; three Solomon boys and a daughter.

On behalf of my beloved sister, I solemnly express:

"I have fought the good fight. I have finished my course. I have kept the faith."

-2 Timothy 4:7, KJV.

About My Sister

My sister, Boi Hawa Kpanabom, (and I) were removed from our home, Kpangbama, Imperri Chiefdom, Bonthe District, to Bo Town, the provincial capital of the Southern Province when we were very young, for the main reason of having the opportunity to attend a good school. Boi Hawa stayed with Mi Maseray, a relative of ours and successful businesswoman. I stayed with Mama Yarkai and her three children, Ngadie, Amara and Umu Fofana at Number 1 Mission Road. Mama Yarkai was still running her Provision Store at Chief Boima's Compound.

My sister had the opportunity of attending a good school to the level of education needed for women in those days. In addition, she acquired proper traditional and cultural training through her close relationship with both Mi Maseray and Mama Yarkai. When she was old enough to be initiated into the Sacred Bondo Society, she returned home. After her initiation, she married Milton Margai who was at that time a political party leader who eventually became Prime Minister, and then Head of State after the Sierra Leone's independence, and finally, was knighted by Her Royal Majesty, Queen Elizabeth II.

I had the opportunity to attend an American Boarding Mission School for boys, Danville, at Kpangbaia, then Centennial Secondary School in Mattru Jong, then briefly at Albert Academy, in Freetown, then I left for Europe for further education. From Europe, I came to Canada as a citizen of the British Commonwealth of Nations. I then moved to St. Catharines and enrolled at Brock University, where I obtained my first degree, then University of Windsor where I obtained my Honours in Business Administration and my Master's Degree.

About the Author

My first attraction at Brock University was the free English lessons organized by the Dean of Students to help foreign students improve on their written and spoken English. I took advantage of that and was able to attend most of the lectures. They were excellent. I also took the opportunity to play some practice soccer games with the Brock Soccer Team, and Club Roma, but I had no intention of joining either team for competitive games.

One Friday afternoon, Dr. Lowenberger, the Dean of Students, called me to his office. I stood in front of his table as he dialed a phone number. He then handed the phone over to me telling me to talk to Doug Court of Court Industries. I did not know what to say, except, "Good afternoon, sir." Mr. Court invited me to his house for breakfast the next day. From that event, Doug and Nancy Court and their children adopted me as a member of their family. They're my Canadian family to this day. Throughout my student days, they assisted me with housing, food, and part-time employment in Court Industries. Whenever there was a shortage of work for students in Court Industries on Bunting Road in St. Catharines, Doug Court would regularly arrange for me to be employed at the Walker's Quarry at Niagara Falls, a place I used to like working at during the summer. The connection I have had with Doug and Nancy Court, and their children, brought improvement and considerable change in my life. That relationship continued to flourish even when I returned to Sierra Leone.

The last time I met Dr. Lowenberger at one of the dinners organized by Brock University, I expressed my gratitude to him for having connected me to the Court Family. I was surprised that he vividly remembered bringing me to his office to talk to Doug Court, because he had previously given me Doug Court's phone number and the phone number of Court Industries, for me to contact them, but I did not call them. So, he made it a point of duty to make that connection for me. What a gentleman! He is awesome.

During my graduate school days at the University of Windsor, I was between the City of Windsor and St. Catharines. I only went to Windsor for my lectures and to play tennis. Windsor by then was a bigger university with lots of facilities, while Brock was one of the newest universities in the Commonwealth and had more help available to foreign students. After graduating from the University of Windsor, I was employed by Canadian National Rail in Toronto at Front Street. I worked there for a few years then I returned home to be reunited with my family after many years of being away. Fortunately, I was present when Mama Hawa was elected Paramount Chief of Imperri Chiefdom.